STUDIES IN ENGLISH LITERATURE NO. 65

General Editor

David Daiches

Professor of English
at the University of Sussex

Already published in the series:

1. **Milton:** Comus *and* Samson Agonistes by *J. B. Broadbent*
2. **Pope:** The Rape of the Lock by *J. S. Cunningham*
3. **Jane Austen:** Emma by *Frank Bradbrook*
4. **W. B. Yeats:** The Poems by *A. Norman Jeffares*
5. **Chaucer:** The Knight's Tale *and* The Clerk's Tale by *Elizabeth Salter*
6. **Marlowe:** Dr Faustus by *Philip Brockbank*
7. **Hardy:** The Mayor of Casterbridge by *Douglas Brown*
8. **Webster:** The Duchess of Malfi by *Clifford Leech*
10. **Wordsworth:** The Prelude and other poems by *John F. Danby*
11. **George Eliot:** Middlemarch by *David Daiches*
12. **Conrad:** Lord Jim by *Tony Tanner*
13. **Shakespeare:** Hamlet by *Kenneth Muir*
14. **Shakespeare:** Macbeth by *John Russell Brown*
15. **Shakespeare:** King Lear by *Nicholas Brooke*
16. **Shakespeare:** Much Ado About Nothing by *J. R. Mulryne*
17. **Donne:** Songs and Sonets by *A. J. Smith*
18. **Marvell:** Poems by *Dennis Davison*
19. **Dickens:** Great Expectations by *R. George Thomas*
20. **Emily Brontë:** Wuthering Heights by *Frank Goodridge*
21. **Shakespeare:** The Merchant of Venice by *A. D. Moody*
22. **Tennyson:** In Memoriam by *K. W. Gransden*
23. **Fielding:** Tom Jones by *I. Ehrenpreis*
24. **Shakespeare:** Henry IV by *R. J. Beck*
25. **Shakespeare:** As You Like It by *Michael Jamieson*
26. **Shakespeare:** The Winter's Tale by *A. D. Nuttall*
28. **D. H. Lawrence:** Sons and Lovers by *Gāmini Salgādo*
29. **Dickens:** Little Dorrit by *J. C. Reid*
30. **E. M. Forster:** A Passage to India by *John Colmer*
31. **Shakespeare:** Richard II by *A. R. Humphreys*
32. **Henry James:** The Portrait of a Lady by *David Galloway*
33. **Gissing:** New Grub Street by *P. J. Keating*
34. **Blake:** The Lyric Poetry by *John Holloway*
35. **Shakespeare:** A Midsummer Night's Dream by *Stephen Fender*
36. **Mark Twain:** Huckleberry Finn by *Jonathan Raban*
37. **T. S. Eliot:** The Waste Land by *Helen Williams (2nd edition)*
38. **Swift:** Gulliver's Travels by *Angus Ross*
39. **Shakespeare:** The Tempest by *John Russell Brown*
40. **Conrad:** Nostromo by *Juliet McLauchlan*
41. **Tennyson:** The Early Poems by *John Pettigrew*
42. **Golding:** Lord of the Flies by *John S. Whitley*

Already published in the series (*continued*):

43. **Hardy:** Tess of the D'Urbervilles
by *Bruce Hugman*
44. **Shakespeare:** Antony and Cleopatra
by *Robin Lee*
45. **Webster:** The White Devil
by *D. C. Gunby*
46. **D. H. Lawrence:** The Rainbow
by *Frank Glover-Smith*
47. **Shakespeare:** Othello
by *Juliet McLauchlan*
48. **Virginia Woolf:** To the Lighthouse
by *Stella McNichol*
49. **Pope:** The Dunciad
by *Howard Erskine-Hill*
50. **James Joyce:** Ulysses
by *Michael Mason*
51. **Tobias Smollett:**
The Expedition of Humphry Clinker
by *John Valdimir Price*
52. **James Joyce:**
A Portrait of the Artist as a Young Man
by *Harvey Peter Sucksmith*
53. **Gerard Manley Hopkins:** The Poems
by *R. K. R. Thornton*
54. **Dickens:** Bleak House
by *Grahame Smith*
55. **Samuel Richardson:** Clarissa
by *Anthony Kearney*
56. **Wordsworth and Coleridge:**
The Lyrical Ballads
by *Stephen Prickett*
57. **Shakespeare:** Measure for Measure
by *Nigel Alexander*
58. **Shakespeare:** Coriolanus
by *Brian Vickers*
59. **Chaucer:** Troilus and Criseyde
by *A. C. Spearing*
60. **F. Scott Fitzgerald:** The Great Gatsby
by *John S. Whitley*
61. **John Gay:** The Beggar's Opera
by *Peter Lewis*
62. **Patrick White:** Voss
by *William Walsh*
63. **Huxley and Orwell:** Brave New World and Nineteen Eighty-Four
by *Jenni Calder*
64. Poetry of the First World War
by *J. M. Gregson*
65. **Shakespeare.** Julius Caesar
by *David Daiches*
66. **Achebe:** Things Fall Apart
by *Kate Turkington*
67. **Dickens:** David Copperfield
by *Philip Collins*
68. **Tourneur:** The Revenger's Tragedy
by *Philip J. Ayres*

SHAKESPEARE: JULIUS CAESAR

by

DAVID DAICHES

EDWARD ARNOLD

First published 1976 by
Edward Arnold (Publishers) Ltd
25 Hill Street, London W1X 8LL

Cloth edition ISBN: 0 7131 5927 8
Paper edition ISBN: 0 7131 5928 6

Printed in Great Britain by
The Camelot Press Ltd, Southampton

General Preface

The object of this series is to provide studies of individual novels, plays and groups of poems and essays which are known to be widely read by students. The emphasis is on clarification and evaluation; biographical and historical facts, while they may be discussed when they throw light on particular elements in a writer's work, are generally subordinated to critical discussion. What kind of work is this? What exactly goes on here? How good is this work, and why? These are the questions that each writer will try to answer.

It should be emphasized that these studies are written on the assumption that the reader has already read carefully the work discussed. The objective is not to enable students to deliver opinions about works they have not read, nor is it to provide ready-made ideas to be applied to works that have been read. In one sense all critical interpretation can be regarded as foisting opinions on readers, but to accept this is to deny the advantages of any sort of critical discussion directed at sudents or indeed at anybody else. The aim of these studies is to provide what Coleridge called in another context 'aids to reflection' about the works discussed. The interpretations are offered as suggestive rather than as definitive, in the hope of stimulating the reader into developing further his own insights. This is after all the function of all critical discourse among sensible people.

Because of the interest which this kind of study has aroused, it has been decided to extend it first from merely English literature to include also some selected works of American literature and now further to include selected works in English by Commonwealth writers. The criterion will remain that the book studied is important in itself and is widely read by students.

DAVID DAICHES

Julius Caesar

In the 1623 Folio edition of Shakespeare's plays, which provides our only text for Julius Caesar, the play is called 'The Tragedie of Iulius Caesar'. This indicates that Shakespeare's contemporaries, and in all likelihood Shakespeare himself, considered the play to be a tragedy. The twelve plays in the Tragedy section of the Folio (which includes all Shakespeare's Roman plays) are so diverse in theme and mood that there might seem to be no point in pursuing the implications of the term 'tragedy' when applied to any given play. Nevertheless, since the folio divides the plays into Comedies, Histories and Tragedies, and puts all the English history plays, including *Richard II* and *Richard III*, among the Histories, the editors must have had some reason for putting the plays dealing with Roman history in the tragedy section other than the simple reason that that principal character meets with his death. (The Second Quarto of *Hamlet*, incidentally, calls itself a 'tragicall historie', but it is doubtful if this has any critical significance.)

Whatever we conclude to have been the Elizabethan and Jacobean view or views of tragedy, it is clear that a Shakespearean tragedy is the tragedy of a person or persons. This is clear enough in plays as diverse as *Romeo and Juliet* and *Hamlet*, but as soon as we ask the question 'whose tragedy?' of *Julius Caesar* we come up against a central point of critical controversy. The play can hardly be the tragedy of Caesar himself, for he is murdered at the beginning of Act III and disappears from the play thereafter except for his brief appearance to Brutus as a ghost in Act IV. And though what Brutus called 'the spirit of Caesar' plays, as we shall see, a significant part in the play, this spirit is something like an idea of political policy, and an idea can't be a tragic hero. A commonly held view is that *Julius Caesar*, in spite of its title (and Shakespeare never bothered much about titles: the play written immediately after *Julius Caesar* was probably *As You Like It*), has Brutus as its tragic hero. On this view Brutus is the sensitive idealist who in his moral innocence and lack of awareness of the practical realities of power-politics kills his best friend from the highest motives and produces in Rome an exacerbated version of the very despotism that killing has been designed to prevent. Supporters of this view cite the many scenes where we see Brutus exhibiting kindness, sensitivity, high moral feeling and disinterested concern for the welfare of the state and quote Antony's concluding remark that 'all the conspirators save only he / Did that they did in envy of great Caesar.' Brutus thus appears as an exemplar of private virtue as opposed to public virtue, his behaviour and his fate illustrating the fact that private virtue cannot in itself cope with the necessities of public life and that, however admirable in a domestic context Brutus may appear, in a public context the very qualities that make him a good private person make him a menace. This, it is argued, is a genuinely tragic insight. There are situations in which virtue can be politically and socially dangerous, and in such situations a shrewd sense of *Realpolitik*, a genuine apprehension of the real motives which inspire men and the most effective way to get them to act, which often goes together with a degree of lack of moral scruple, is what best serves the public welfare. Both Cassius, who proceeds against Caesar from personal jealousy but who knows just what he is doing and what ought to be done if the assassination of Caesar is to result in the consequences he wishes, and Antony, who combines personal passion with a cool ability to manipulate the passions of others in his own interest, are morally inferior though politically superior to Brutus. Octavius, a cold fish who conducts himself with a quiet awareness of his own interests which he identifies with those of the state, emerges at the end as the natural restorer of order and thus, while far from the ideal man morally, is the effective practical man whom his country needs.

Such an interpretation would construe *Julius Caesar* as a politico-moral play about the relation between virtue and power. That there is an element of this in the play can hardly be denied. But to read it simply in this way is to impose an abstractness on its concrete details that does violence to the play's achieved reality. It is also to beg a central question: how are we to interpret Caesar? For Shakespeare's presentation of Caesar in the play is capable of a variety of interpretations: a great deal depends on what view of Caesar he was taking for granted among his audience when he put in the individualizing touches that could be seen equally as humanizing a legendary hero or showing that legendary hero to be no hero at all but a petty-minded and tyrannical boaster.

There were two diametrically opposed views of Caesar available to Shakespeare, and these may be roughly described as the medieval view, which saw the Roman Empire as the divinely appointed vehicle for the conversion of Europe to Christianity and the murder of Julius Caesar as a wicked attempt to forestall the establishment of the Empire, and the Renaissance view, which saw the Republic as the great age of Rome and the Empire as degenerate and immoral. On the first view, Caesar was a hero and Brutus and Cassius, his murderers, were deep-dyed villains, as they were, for example, in the view of Dante, who put them in the lowest circle of Hell beside Judas Iscariot. On the second view Caesar was a tyrant and his murderers were liberators. Both views of Caesar have been attributed to Shakespeare by different critics. Shakespeare got the bulk of his material for his play from North's translation of Plutarch's *Lives* of Caesar, Brutus and Antony, and it might be thought that Plutarch's view of Caesar would provide a clue as to how Shakespeare saw him. But Plutarch shows both good and bad in Caesar, portraying him, as he also portrayed Brutus and Cassius, 'with a mixture of approval and disapproval' (in Geoffrey Bullough's words), so that we cannot infer from Plutarch's view what attitude to Caesar Shakespeare took for granted among his audience. To solve this, as to solve all other problems of interpretation, we must look to the text of the play itself, though it will also be helpful occasionally to look at the way Shakespeare uses his source material.

The play opens in rhetoric:

> Hence! home, you idle creatures, get you home!
> Is this a holiday?

Flavius and Marullus, the tribunes of the people, are berating 'certain commoners' (as the Folio's stage direction calls them) of Rome for celebrating Caesar's triumph and forgetting the glories of Pompey, whom Caesar had defeated and who was subsequently murdered. The question 'Is this a holiday?' is purely rhetorical: Flavius does not pause for an answer but goes on to attack the commoners for not wearing the appropriate costumes of their trade on an ordinary working day:

> What, know you not,
> Being mechanical [workers], you ought not walk
> Upon a labouring day without the sign
> Of your profession?

'The ordered society in Shakespeare', Northrop Frye has remarked, 'is, to use Heidegger's term, ecstatic: its members are outside themselves, at work in the world, and their being is their function.'[1] Flavius's speech is thus a profession of belief in the ordered society: it is a sign of disorder that men should abandon their work and the visible signs of their calling to 'cull out a holiday' when they have no right to a holiday. Flavius and Marullus in this opening scene therefore seem to be suggesting that Caesar is a threat to the ordered state (for it is to celebrate Caesar that the commoners have gone on holiday). Yet by the time they come to mention Caesar and explain their indignation, it is not Caesar as a cause of disorder who emerges, but Caesar the man 'that comes in triumph over Pompey's blood'. And at the end of the scene, when the two tribunes are left alone, Flavius complains of Caesar's inordinate ambition that 'would keep us all in servile fearfulness'. But before we reach this point Marullus, in a set rhetorical piece, laments the dead Pompey and reproves the commoners for honouring Pompey's conqueror:

> Wherefore rejoice? What conquests brings he home?
> What tributaries follow him to Rome
> To grace in captive bonds his chariot wheels?
> You blocks, you stones, you worse than senseless things!
> O you hard hearts, you cruel men of Rome!
> Knew you not Pompey?

The speech continues with a vivid evocation of the people of Rome waiting all day 'to see great Pompey pass the streets of Rome' and raising 'an universal shout' on his apperance, to move into another series of questions:

> And do you now put on your best attire?
> And do you now cull out a holiday?
> And do you now strew flowers in his way
> That comes in triumph over Pompey's blood?

And they are told to go home and beg forgiveness from the gods for such ingratitude. When they are gone, Flavius suggests to Marullus that he should remove the ornaments from Caesar's statues while he himself will 'drive away the vulgar from the streets', concluding:

[1] 'The Tragedy of Order: *Julius Caesar*', in *Fools of Time*, London, 1965.

These growing feathers plucked from Caesar's wing
Will make him fly an ordinary pitch
Who else would soar above the view of men
And keep us all in servile fearfulness.

This opening movement of the play is complex. First, we have the introduction of the order-disorder theme, which is to wind in and out of the play and provoke a number of paradoxes: Caesar's dictatorial ambition is against the proper order of the state and provokes disorder; yet his murder will produce the ultimate in rioting, lynching and civil war, and order will finally be restored only by the restoration of 'the spirit of Caesar' in his nephew and heir Octavius. Then we get the prose dialogue between Flavius, Marullus and the Cobbler, in which the cobbler shows himself good-humoured and witty—a very different view of the common man of Rome from that which will emerge after Antony's rhetoric has done its work following Caesar's murder. Then comes Marullus's speech with its elegiac evocation of great Pompey, once loved and honoured, now dead and ignored while his conqueror is acclaimed. And finally we have the tribunes' determination to clip Caesar's wings for fear of having to live under him in 'servile fearfulness'.

There is another point worth noting. 'You blocks, you stones, you worse than senseless things!' exclaims Marullus to the commoners of Rome. But later, when Antony speaks to these people, he says quite the reverse: 'You are not wood, you are not stones, but men.' Now it is true that both descriptions are part of set rhetorical pieces—and, as we shall see, set rhetorical pieces play an unusually important part in this play—and are not therefore to be taken as representing an objective statement of fact or even the genuine views of the speakers. But to a critic looking at the unfolding action and language of the play in order to find the fully realized meaning of the whole such a contrast is surely instructive. It is part of the deliberate denial in the play of any simple or single moral or psychological or political judgement. The celebrating commoners represent disorder. They have forgotten Pompey and are ungrateful to him by celebrating Caesar. (But why should they be grateful to Pompey? What did he ever do for them except provide a public show? Later Antony is to tell the crowd of specific things that Caesar did for them.) Caesar is ambitious and ought to be restrained. These sentiments voiced by the tribunes are curiously unrelated. It is as though they are seeking for a reason for their uneasiness without being able to put their finger on it precisely. Yet it is surely significant that the final words of the scene are not about the threat of disorder or about regret for the dead Pompey but express fear of Caesar's dictatorial intentions. It is with the expression of this fear in our ears that we see the ceremonial entry of Caesar on to the stage and first hear his voice. (It is important to remember that in Shakespeare's theatre there was no break between scenes: the stage empties with the departure of Flavius and Marullus, and almost immediately afterwards Caesar and his train enter.)

We have already heard from Marullus that it is the feast of Lupercal, on which occasion, as Shakespeare learned from North's translation of Plutarch, young men ran through the city 'striking in sport them they meet in the way' while pregnant women or barren women wishing to become pregnant offered themselves to the strikers in the belief that being struck would bring them either an easy birth or the assurance of future pregnancy. Plutarch does not say that Caesar ordered his wife to stand in the way of Antony as he ran the course in order that she might be touched by him and 'shake off' her sterility, but in fact this is the very first thing Shakespeare has Caesar say once he has brought him on the stage. His very first word is his wife's name, 'Calphurnia' (North's and Shakespeare's spelling of Calpurnia) pronounced in a tone of command. No sooner has he spoken it than Casca cries 'Peace ho! Caesar speaks', thus silencing all other sounds (including music) and focussing attention on Caesar as the great man. Caesar tells Calphurnia to stand in Antony's way when he runs and then turns to Antony (evoking from him the obsequious 'Caesar, my lord?') to tell him to touch Calphurnia

for our elders say
The barren, touched in this holy chase,
Shake off their sterile curse.

It is a strange introduction of the powerful conqueror whose threat to Roman liberty has already been expressed by Flavius. Is Shakespeare lowering him in our estimation by showing him as superstitious? Or does the phrase 'our elders say' suggest that he himself is sceptical of what is merely a traditional belief? Caesar goes on to tell Antony to 'leave no ceremony out'. This particular ceremony is not one which exalts Caesar. (Contrast Plutarch describing this same scene: 'Caesar sat to behold that sport upon the pulpit for orations, in a chair of gold, apparelled in triumphing manner.') Yet the attention and deference paid to Caesar, the sounding of his name seven times in twenty-four lines (as Granville-Barker has pointed out) leaves no doubt of his dominant position in the scene.

It is while we are resolving the mixed impressions of Caesar as superstitious, as sceptical and as the centre of deferential attention that his name is pronounced by the soothsayer: silence is again called for, and Caesar shows himself aware of the special nature of the call by his highly formal reply:

> Who is it in the press that calls on me?
> I hear a tongue shriller than all the music
> Cry 'Caesar!' Speak. Caesar is turned to hear.

He speaks of himself in the third person—a habit we are to see more of. The soothsayer tells him to beware the ides of March, and he repeats the warning when, at Caesar's order, he is set face to face with the great man. 'A soothsayer bids you beware the ides of March,' says Brutus helpfully—the first words he speaks in the play, oddly banal, yet, in the light of what is to happen on the ides of March and of Brutus's as yet unplanned role in that happening (which must have been known to the audience, even those seeing the play for the first time), carrying an ironic *frisson*. On the soothsayer's repeating the warning before Caesar's face, it looks as though a dramatic confrontation is about to build up. But no: in a curt speech containing two imperatives Caesar dismisses the man:

> He is a dreamer. Let us leave him. Pass.

The trumpet sounds, and he moves off the stage with his train, leaving on the stage only Brutus and Cassius.

We are left with no certain impression of Caesar. The confident dismissal of the soothsayer and his warning suggests a certain authority and imperviousness to superstition, but his earlier orders to Calphurnia and Antony suggests that he is (or may very well be) superstitious. His actual position in Roman society, seen as threatening 'servile fearfulness' by Flavius, is suggested rather than presented. We remember Antony's deferential 'When Caesar says "Do this," it is performed', but it is not yet clear whether this may not tell us more about Antony than about Caesar. Yet, fragmentary though this initial picture of Caesar is, and totally inconclusive about his character, he is not shown as a cypher. He seems to be a man acting a part, but the very uncertainty in the character he is playing suggests a real and complex man underneath. The play never does more than suggest the existence of such a man, and for this reason alone it cannot be said to be Caesar's tragedy, however important a part he plays implicitly in the total pattern of its action.

Caesar and his train are to return later in the same scene, but meanwhile, punctuating his two appearances, we have the dialogue between the two men long traditionally known, in either condemnation or admiration, as the prime conspirators against him. It is important to stress here that Shakespeare is dealing with known facts: though the details of Caesar's life and death were not as well known to the mass of his audience as the facts he drew on in his English history plays, the names of Brutus and Cassius as leaders in the conspiracy to assassinate Caesar must have been familiar to most people who were likely to attend the Globe theatre (where *Julius Caesar* was probably first performed). So when we are presented for the first time with these two talking confidentially together we are immediately on the alert. What sort of characters are they and what have they to say about Caesar? This is not only a legitimate dramatic question: it is an essential one. In the twentieth-century reaction against A. C. Bradley's concentration on the psychological make-up of Shakespeare's characters in favour of seeing the plays in terms of their total structure as integrated dramatic poems, it is sometimes forgotten that Shakespeare's dramatic technique often *invites* us to inquire into character and motivation and that the pattern of meaning of the play depends on the projection of an awareness of what sort of people certain characters are and why they act as they do. Certainly the dialogue that Shakespeare now presents us with is meant to illuminate the character and motives of both Brutus and Cassius. The moral and political implications of their being what they are and behaving as they will behave are another matter. These implications are an important part of the total meaning of the play, but they are not spelled out, but rather echo away into reverberating suggestions.

Brutus resists Cassius's suggestion that he 'go see the order of the course'. (It is clear from what follows that Cassius had no desire that Brutus should go, and knew that by asking the question he would provoke not only a refusal but also an explanation on Brutus's part of why his nature was averse to such sports, which in turn would give Cassius an opening for a discussion of the threat posed by Caesar.) Brutus

.. There is no suggestion that Brutus is especially touched by f argument (the actor playing Brutus should perhaps look at th slight puzzlement during this part of his speech), but, sing this, Cassius then hits on a point that he knows will come me to Brutus:

you and I have heard our fathers say
re was a Brutus once that would have brooked
eternal devil to keep his state in Rome
easily as a king.

s the ultimate bad word for Brutus, whose ancestor Lucius itus, as he himself boasts in II, i, 53–4, 'did from the streets of he Tarquin drive when he was called a king'. The reference to ancestor expelling Tarquin and so founding the Roman has more effect than the comparisons of names or the anger at greatness. Brutus now replies soberly and at first in a private t he is aware what Cassius is getting at and will think about it. annot stay in the private mode long in dealing with such a nd he ends his speech with another rhetorical reference to the third person:

utus had rather be a villager
ian to repute himself a son of Rome
nder these hard conditions as this time
like to lay upon us.

and his train now return, with Caesar looking angry, nia pale, 'and all the rest look like a chidden train'. We hear alking to Antony, complaining of Cassius's 'lean and hungry d of his thinking too much. 'Fear him not, Caesar,' says Antony, sar replies:

Vould he were fatter! But I fear him not.
'et if my name were liable to fear,
do not know the man I should avoid
o soon as that same Cassius.

akespeare is deliberately, perhaps even playfully, setting side by human Caesar and Caesar the role-taking dictator. He goes on to n Cassius's ironic and ascetic character, so unlike Antony:

is very ready to insist on the seriousness of his own character, especially in contrast with that of Antony:

I am not gamesome. I do lack some part
Of that quick spirit that is Antony.

Cassius welcomes the introduction of the subject of Brutus's character, and it does not take him long before he has Brutus confessing his inward perplexity:

Vexed I am
Of late with passions of some difference [i.e., conflicting emotions],
Conceptions only proper to myself, . . .

Only proper to himself? If they had remained so, there would have been no tragedy. As we shall see, one of Brutus's problems was that he could not easily distinguish between passions proper to himself and those relevant to a public situation. Even when he talks about himself in a tone of self-pity he is capable of talking of himself in the third person (as Caesar does, for different reasons). His friends must not be grieved

Nor construe any further my neglect
Than that poor Brutus, with himself at War,
Forgets the show of love to other men.

The slow, plangent tone of these lines is very much in the Brutus idiom. It is part of his charm (as what Wilson Knight called the 'Othello music' is part of the charm of Othello when he is truly himself): there is a concerned brooding sadness in many of his speeches, when he talks to his wife or to his servant Lucius as well as when he talks to and of himself. Cassius does not give him time to develop this tone. He intervenes to suggest that Brutus cannot really see himself as others see him: he does not appreciate his own 'hidden worthiness' nor is he aware that

many of the best respect in Rome
(Except immortal Caesar), speaking of Brutus
And groaning underneath this age's yoke,
Had wished that noble Brutus had his eyes.

Now it is out: Cassius wants Brutus to share his view of 'this age's yoke'. Brutus is startled to hear the matter put so bluntly and, in a quite different tone of voice, asks

> Into what dangers would you lead me, Cassius,
> That you would have me seek into myself
> For that which is not in me?

But it *is* in him, as Cassius undertakes to show. He is interrupted by a 'flourish and shout', and Brutus reacts as Cassius wants him to:

> What means this shouting? I do fear the people
> Choose Caesar for their king.

Cassius pounces on that word 'fear' in order to force Brutus to admit that he 'would not have it so'.

So far, we have been shown little of the character and motives of Cassius, except indirectly. We have the remarkable spectacle of Cassius persuading Brutus to join in some kind of movement against Caesar without Cassius himself saying what he thinks of the matter at all. He professes to be merely holding a mirror up to Brutus and showing him the Brutus that other people see. By this method he has got Brutus to admit that he would not wish to see Caesar king, 'yet I love him well'. He has also got him to mount his high moral-rhetorical horse and ride on it towards the goal that Cassius wants him to reach:

> What is it that you would impart to me?
> If it be aught toward the general good,
> Set honour in one eye and death i' th' other,
> And I will look on both indifferently;
> For let the gods so speed me as I love
> The name of honour more than I fear death.

He is talking about himself, and in highly abstract terms. He loves 'the name of honour' more than he fears death. This is the language of public rhetoric, not of inward debate. Now we must not be too censorious about this. We know that it was an accepted convention of Shakespeare's stage that characters can talk of their own virtue in a purely informative way, without being accused of egotism. Nevertheless, Brutus's sliding away from the particular question of the state of Rome to talk about honour and death is characteristic of him. This is part of his 'nobility'. He

is shown in the play as possessing a
dealing with moral and political
abstractness of his inward argument in
10 ff.) demonstrates conclusively; yet he
directly with individuals, especially i
melancholy in them. His two modes a
How different is Cassius's mode, as app
replies to Brutus's talk of honour and d
glad you said that, for 'honour is the su
goes on to express, in excited, irascible v
Caesar, whom he once had to rescue fro
had challenged him to join in swimming
much more powerful than himself. The t
anger. He goes on to describe how he onc
in Spain. ' 'Tis true, this god did shake.'
the shaking was due to fever, he goes on,
to cowardice: 'His coward lips did from t
fever Caesar had to ask Titinius for a dri
stuttering with rage. Honour is not the s
raging with jealousy:

> Ye gods, it doth ama
> A man of such a feeble temper shou
> So get the start of the majestic worl
> And bear the palm alone.

He is interrupted by another shout and fl
express the fear that some new honours
provoke Cassius to an even stronger outbu
share his outrage at the *disparity* between C
their own.

> 'Brutus' and 'Caesar'. What should b
> Why should that name be sounded m

He goes on to compare the two *names*, concl
the other. This is the expression of something
a sense of absolute outrage that one man sho
the same class, and a kind of genuine eg
through his language (egalitarian, that is, w

social clas
this kind
Cassius w
perhaps se
forcibly h

> O
> Th
> Th
> As

'King' w
Junius B
Rome / T
Brutus's
Republic
Caesar's
voice, th
But he
subject,
himself

> F
> T
> U
> I

Caesa
Calphu
Caesar
look' a
and Ca

Here
side th
dwell

Such men as he be never at heart's ease
Whiles they behold a greater than themselves,
And therefore are they very dangerous.
I rather tell thee what is to be feared
Than what I fear; for always I am Caesar.
Come on my right side, for this ear is deaf,
And tell me truly what thou think'st of him.

We already know that he is quite right about Cassius. But as we are admiring Caesar's astuteness we see him passing again from the ordinary human to the symbolic superman, only to return again with remarkable swiftness to the fallible human with one deaf ear. The contrast at this point is positively startling. Is Shakespeare de-bunking Caesar? Or is he simply showing that the man and the symbol can co-exist in the same person? Or (as seems most likely) is he leaving the question open?

Caesar departs very much an ordinary man, including his one good ear to hear Antony's opinion of Cassius. Yet his exit with his train is at the same time ceremonial: 'Sennet. Exeunt Caesar and his Train' reads the Folio stage direction. (A sennet is a set of notes on the trumpet, used for ceremonial purposes.) We are left with Brutus and Cassius again—but now they are joined by Casca, whom they detain as he is about to leave with the others in order to learn exactly what had been happening when they heard the shouts go up. Casca describes, in blunt and cynical prose that deliberately degrades the events he is describing, how Caesar was three times offered a crown by Antony and three times declined it, but each time more reluctantly than the time before. And in the end he fell down in an epileptic fit (the 'falling sickness'). The tone of Casca's narrative throughout is contemptuous of Caesar, yet as Cassius has already remarked on Casca's 'sour fashion' of speech, it is left open to us to see Casca's account as unrealistically prejudicial. Shakespeare is leaving as many points open as he can. It is interesting that when we see Casca again, in the following scene, he is no longer the blunt cynical observer with a sour fashion of speech, but a frightened and superstitious simpleton. Shakespeare did not always trouble to be consistent with minor characters when he was using them simply to carry on the action or to illuminate situations in which other characters were the principal actors.

There is another example of Shakespeare's deliberate ambiguity in the scene with Brutus, Cassius and Casca. Casca tells the other two that 'Marullus and Flavius, for pulling scarfs off Caesar's images, are put to silence.' Plutarch says only that Caesar 'deprived Marullus and Flavius of their Tribuneships'. Shakespeare's choice of an ambiguous phrase—and it is amusing to see generations of editors competing in offering different explanations of it—when his source provided him with something quite specific cannot be accidental. The phrase 'put to silence' suggests some dread and secret penalty imposed by an arbitrary authority.

Casca and then Brutus depart, leaving Cassius alone on the stage to reveal in a rather wooden soliloquy that he has been deliberately manipulating Brutus:

> Well, Brutus, thou art noble; yet I see
> Thy honourable mettle may be wrought
> From that it is disposed . . .
> Caesar doth bear me hard; but he loves Brutus.
> If I were Brutus now and he were Cassius,
> He should not humour me.

Cassius is using the terms 'noble' and 'honourable' (the latter of which Antony is to use so effectively in his oration over Caesar's body) if not ironically then at least, as it were, in inverted commas. Brutus, Plutarch tells has, 'framed his manner of life by the rules of virtue and study of philosophy. . . . So that his very enemies which wish him most hurt, because of his conspiracy against Julius Caesar, if there were any noble attempt done in all this conspiracy, they refer it wholly unto Brutus, and all the cruel and violent acts unto Cassius, who was Brutus's familiar friend but not so well given and conditioned as he.' At this point in the play it may seem that Shakespeare is simply accepting the view here put forward by Plutarch. But by the time the play's pattern is completed it is clear that such a simplified view will not do. Yet it is *part* of the play's truth, and it is significant that Shakespeare leaves his audience with this impression at the end of the first encounter between Brutus and Cassius.

The scene between Cassius and Casca that follows shows Cassius—who follows the philosophy of Epicurus and does not himself believe in omens and prognostications—successfully impressing on the frightened Casca that the thunder and lightening and other unusual phenomena suggest the tyranny of Caesar. He presents the case against

Caesar very differently from the way he did to Brutus, for Casca is a very different character, but equally effectively. His speech beginning 'I know where I will wear this dagger then' is almost a parody of Stoic rhetoric. (He too is led to speak of himself in the third person. 'Cassius from bondage will deliver Cassius.' Throughout the play when characters do this it suggests that they have fallen into a particular role to achieve a specific purpose.) Yet his rhetoric is different from that of Brutus and equally different from the rhetoric we are later to get from Antony. The varieties of rhetoric employed in the play, and the dramatic purpose served by each, are worth careful study.

Act I concludes with agreement between Cassius, Casca and Cinna that any successful attack on Caesar would have to have the co-operation of Brutus. Casca gives the reason precisely:

> O, he sits high in all the people's hearts;
> And that which would appear offence in us,
> His countenance, like richest alchemy,
> Will change to virtue and to worthiness.

Cassius has decided on various means of persuading Brutus, including leaving letters supposed to come from different citizens of Rome. The act's last words are:

> ere day
> We will awake him and be sure of him.

Brutus is a character manipulated, an instrument. How in fact will he react to Cassius's manipulation? Act II brings us at once to the answer. (It is worth noting that while the scene divisions are the work of later editors, the act divisions are in the Folio text.)

Act II opens with Brutus alone and, after a brief interlude with his servant-boy Lucius (who is used intermittently to establish Brutus's humanity in his relations with his dependents), we are given the soliloquy in which he persuades himself of the necessity to kill Caesar. We already know that (a) Brutus is self-consciously virtuous; (b) his reputation is such that his support of an enterprise will give it public respectability; (c) he has a tendency to rhetorical abstraction (later to be contrasted with Antony's gift for rhetorical concreteness) in discussing moral questions; (d) Cassius regards him as someone who can be manipulated, but also as someone supremely worth manipulating. How will such a person, now quite alone, reveal his inmost thoughts about his friend Caesar?

It is startling to find that before the soliloquy begins he has already made up his mind that Caesar must be killed. That is, this soliloquy does not show Brutus arguing himself into the conclusion that Caesar must be killed: it shows him decided that Caesar must be killed, then going on to justify that decision by tortuous abstract arguments. Six leaden monosyllables open the speech:

> It must be by his death

We must imagine a fairly long pause before he goes on to add

> and for my part
> I know no personal cause to spurn at him,
> But for the general.

The public interest demands the killing of the man who is his personal friend and against whom he has no personal grudge. He must be killed because 'he would be crowned' and

> How that might change his nature, there's the question.

All he knows for fact so far is that Caesar has three times rejected a crown, but he takes it as a fact that 'he would be crowned', after which his nature *might* be changed, and once changed he might become dangerous. So far everything in his argument is hypothetical. He goes on:

> Th'abuse of greatness is, when it disjoins
> Remorse from power. And to speak truth of Caesar
> I have not known when his affections swayed
> More than his reason.

Power becomes dangerous when its wielder puts aside all 'remorse' (mercy). Yet he has never known Caesar ruled by his passions rather than by reason. But, he now goes on to say, ' 'tis common proof' (that is, it is a fact proved by common experience) that a man's character can change when he gets to the top of ambition's ladder. It is possible, then, that if Caesar is crowned king, his character may change:

> Then lest he may, prevent.

This is the nub of an astonishingly hypothetical argument. He concludes by saying quite specifically that, since the kind of person Caesar actually is can provide no ground for killing him, we must find such ground by assuming that his character is going to change:

> And since the quarrel
> Will bear no colour for the thing he is,
> Fashion it thus: that what he is, augmented,
> Would run to these and these extremities;
> And therefore think him as a serpent's egg,
> Which hatched, would as his kind grow mischievous,
> And kill him in the shell.

One knows that serpents' eggs do inevitably produce serpents when hatched; so if we imagine Caesar to be a serpent's egg (which he is not: he is a man) we shall be justified in killing him in the shell before he emerges as a serpent.

It is an extraordinary exercise in what the old grammar books called an 'unfulfilled condition in the future tense'. If we are meant to take this soliloquy as providing the real reasons why Brutus has decided to join in the murder of Caesar, then we must conclude that his judgement about public affairs has an almost fanatical abstractness about it. Had Brutus then another reason, which led him to come to this conclusion before he embarked on this tortuous piece of abstract logic? He is certainly not moved by any personal grudge, spite or envy, as Cassius is. All the evidence right through the play contradicts this. It may be that Shakespeare is simply illustrating what happens to a man—and a good man—when he 'frames his manners of life by the rules of virtue and study of philosophy', as Plutarch had put it. Was Shakespeare thinking of those phrases *rules* of virtue and *study* of philosophy, and showing what happens if abstract rules and theoretical study replace spontaneous human feeling? There is a suggestion of this, here and elsewhere in the play. But there is also the suggestion that Cassius's argument about an earlier Brutus having rid Rome of its last king had sunk deep. It was the function of a Brutus to rid the country of a tyrant: his honour and his truth to his ancestry are at stake. It emerges later that Brutus wants to have Caesar killed in a ritual gesture, an abstract symbolic act, and when he finds that it is in fact a bloody business he tries to ritualize the blood.

But perhaps Caesar's murder is a 'good thing', and Shakespeare is taking for granted that his audience knows this? In this case, would not Brutus's explanations of his motives be less important, since we know that in any case he is going to do something politically beneficial? To this we can only answer that this is not what the play in any way says or suggests. Quite apart from any view we may have of the revulsion of Shakespeare and his audience against the assassination of a head of state (Richard III was a special case, and already a legendary monster by Shakespeare's day) the play clearly shows how absolutely wrong *politically* it was to murder Caesar. Was it necessarily wrong morally? What is politically disastrous may be achieved by persons who are privately good, but their goodness does not prevent the act from being morally wrong. The play seems to say this too. We are back to the question of private and public morality again. But the play warns us against posing the question too abstractly. Brutus may be privately a good man who joins in commiting a public crime for reasons connected with his private virtue, but that private virtue itself is mingled with a tendency to regard himself as a public institution, so that the whole private-public contrast is blurred.

However Brutus came to his decision, it is made clear that he did not find it easy. He speaks of his sleeplessness and internal conflict just before he is visited at home by Cassius and fellow conspirators. When Cassius tells him that the conspirators are with him, 'their faces buried in their cloaks', Brutus breaks into a new kind of rhetoric:

> O conspiracy
> Sham'st thou to show thy dang'rous brow by night,
> When evils are most free? O, then by day
> Where wilt thou find a cavern dark enough
> To mask thy monstrous visage? Seek none, conspiracy.
> Hide it in smiles and affability: . . .

The honest man is getting ready to act a part, to play the hypocrite, and he must prepare himself with high histrionic speech in which conspiracy is personified. Personification is generally regarded as the opposite of abstractness, since it is the making of the abstract concrete. But here the personification of conspiracy, and the talk of its masking its monstrous visage in smiles and affability, have a curiously abstract effect, drawing the imagination away from the human reality of what is about to be done.

That human reality is precisely what Brutus cannot help wanting to obscure. He objects to Cassius's proposal that the conspirators should take an oath of resolution on the grounds that this is a unique compact between honesty and honesty (not, interestingly enough, between honest men and honest men) and, unlike all other sorts of conspiracy, does not require an oath. When Cassius suggests bringing in Cicero, Brutus impatiently brushes the suggestion away, 'For he will never follow anything / That other men begin' (is this a glimmer of political realism, or a sole touch of jealousy?). When Decius and Cassius argue for the elimination of Antony as well as Caesar, Brutus dismisses their case on the grounds that that would be real murder, whereas they are going to kill Caesar as 'sacrificers, not butchers'. It is an extraordinary piece of dressing up:

> We all stand up against the spirit of Caesar,
> And in the spirit of men there is no blood.
> O that we then could come by Caesar's spirit
> And not dismember Caesar! But, alas,
> Caesar must bleed for it! And, gentle friends,
> Let's kill him boldly but not wrathfully;
> Let's carve him as a dish fit for the gods,
> Not hew him as a carcass fit for hounds.
> And let our hearts, as subtle masters do,
> Stir up their servants to an act of rage
> And after seem to chide 'em.

The murder of Caesar must be done as a disinterested ritual act. *As a murder it must not be real.* At the same time there must be an element of hypocrisy in it (and we remember the etymology of the word 'hypocrisy' from the Greek *hypocrisis*, 'an acting on the stage'), since after stirring up their hearts to commit the deed, they must 'after *seem* to chide 'em'. If they do it this way, the populace will see them as 'purgers, not murderers'. The audience must surely by now have an intense curiosity as to just how this man, who talks of sacrificing and carving and purging when he is about to join in committing a political murder, will actually behave during and immediately after the assassination.

Cassius is still afraid that it would be a mistake to spare Antony, but Brutus for a second time dismisses his fear in a tone (unusual for him) of confident contempt, and Trebonius agrees with him. Cassius cannot press the matter further. Indeed, at every crisis in the play where Cassius's shrewder practical judgement confronts Brutus's abstracting idealism, it is Cassius who has to give way. He can manipulate Brutus up to a point, but—and this is made abundantly clear in later developments—he cannot help recognizing him as the superior moral character and submitting to his judgement in the end. That is a central element in the tragedy.

We get a glimpse of a superstitious, flattery-loving Caesar when Decius Brutus explains how he can persuade him to come to the Capitol even if he has decided to stay at home (but this is of course a picture through hostile eyes). Then the conspirators disperse, but not before Brutus has once again put the case for hypocrisy:

> Good gentlemen, look fresh and merrily.
> Let not our looks put on our purposes,
> But bear it as our Roman actors do,
> With untired spirits and formal constancy.

The paradox of Brutus, the soul of honour and nobility, pleading for hypocrisy has farreaching implications. Brutus wants to turn a murder into a formal ritual, and in a formal ritual the performer does not act as an individual but as an actor. But what happens to the formal role of the priest if the animal at whose sacrifice he is presiding is actually a formidable human rival who is being killed to prevent his perpetuating supreme power? Is Brutus, in fact, trying to combine two wholly incompatible roles?

Brutus is left alone, and on finding the boy Lucius fast asleep speaks a few of those warmly human lines which bring us back to the true private Brutus at the very point when he has soared almost beyond our ken. Then comes the famous scene with his wife Portia, who reproaches him for keeping his troubled thoughts from her and eventually wrings from him two-and-a-half plangent, slow-moving lines that represent the true Brutus music:

> You are my true and honourable wife,
> As dear to me as are the ruddy drops
> That visit this sad heart.

Then Caius Ligarius enters, the sick man, who assures Brutus that whatever is afoot if Brutus is a leader in the enterprise it is bound to be honourable, so he will join, and discard his sickness. The scene ends with Brutus as public figure again, and this time as leader. 'It is sufficient that Brutus leads me on,' says Caius, and Brutus replies, 'Follow me then.'

The next scene shows Caesar and Calphurnia and parallels the scene between Brutus and Portia. Bad dreams and natural portents have terrified Calphurnia and she pleads with Caesar not to go forth that day. At first Caesar responds with his third-person Caesar-language. 'Caesar shall go forth', and so on. When he is told that the augurers have failed to find a heart in the sacrified beast, he exclaims:

> Caesar should be a beast without a heart
> If he should stay at home today for fear.
> No, Caesar shall not. Danger knows full well
> That Caesar is more dangerous than he.
> We are two lions littered in one day,
> And I the elder and more terrible.
> And Caesar shall go forth.

He mentions his own name four times in seven lines. Is this exhibiting vainglorious self-assertiveness, or is it to be construed as the proper speech for a man of high political power and authority? At least it can be said to be the speech of a man who is *conscious* of possessing high power and authority, and that a man should be conscious of possessing what he in fact does possess and should speak in a style appropriate to that consciousness is not necessarily blameworthy. In spite of his high formal statement that he will indeed go forth, he relents when Calphurnia restates her fears and pleas. For her sake he will stay at home. Is Caesar here being held up as inconsistent and weak? Or is he being shown as a considerate and compassionate husband who can drop his public role and revert to a private one when his human feelings are touched? When Decius Brutus arrives and easily persuades him to revert to his original determination to go forth by painting a picture of the Senate mocking him for basing his behaviour on his wife's dreams, re-expounding the most sinister of those dreams in a favourable way, and pointing out that the Senate have decided to offer Caesar a crown that very day and might change their minds if he did not come, it seems fairly clear that this second change of mind is something less than admirable. Yet the urgently personal tone of affection in which Decius concludes his speech is worth noting:

Pardon me, Caesar; for my dear dear love
To your proceeding bids me tell you this,
And reason to my love is liable.

The play reverberates with professions of love and friendship, and has several instances of the use of the word 'lover' in the sense of warm friend. These words sound ironically in a context of betrayal, murder and the cynical pursuit of self-interest.

In response to Decius, Caesar first turns to Calphurnia in a tone of friendly domestic reproof.

How foolish do your fears seem now, Calphurnia!

Then he resumes his high formal tone:

Give me my robe, for I will go.

Then Brutus and other conspirators enter, and Caesar greets them in a tone which combines genuine friendliness with formal courtesy. It is just the right tone for a powerful public man addressing friends:

Welcome, Publius.
What, Brutus, are you stirred so early too?
Good morrow, Casca. Caius Ligarius,
Caesar was ne'er so much your enemy
As that same ague which had made you lean.

It is important to remember that Caius Ligarius (and Brutus and Cassius too for that matter) had been on Pompey's side in the war between Caesar and Pompey but had been won over by Caesar's friendship and good-will after Pompey's death.

The scene continues to generate an air of combined friendliness and high courtesy. Caesar asks Brutus the time, and when he is answered replies 'I thank you for your pains and courtesy.' Antony enters, and is greeted with a half-humorous reference to his habit of staying up late at nocturnal revels. Then he turns to the others:

Now, Cinna. Now, Metellus. What, Trebonius;
I have an hour's talk in store for you;
Remember that you call on me today;
Be near me, that I may remember you.

They are, of course, to be only too near, as Trebonius cannot help grimly muttering to himself in an aside. The friendly sociability of the occasion is sealed and formalized when Caesar invites them all to take wine with him before they proceed together to the Capitol:

> Good friends, go in and taste some wine with me,
> And we (like friends) will straightway go together.

Drinking together is the elemental ritual of friendship, as Brutus, that great ritualizer, very well knows. He can hardly bear to see the ritual of friendship being conducted in all innocence by the destined victim of a ritual of sacrifice. He comments to himself in anguish on Caesar's use of the phrase 'like friends';

> That every like is not the same, O Caesar,
> The heart of Brutus earns [grieves] to think upon.

The stage empties. Then Artemidorus enters (we are now on the streets of Rome) with his petition warning Caesar against the conspirators. Then he leaves, and the anxious Portia enters with Lucius, bidding him go to the Senate House and report on what is going on. Brutus has told her of the plot (we need not worry that if we work out the practical details we see that there can have been no opportunity for them to talk together again after the end of their last conversation: Shakespeare knew what was effective on the stage), and she is in a state of high agitation. The soothsayer enters, seeking a place where he can stand and present his petition to Caesar as he passes, and his announced intention of doing this increases Portia's anxiety. It is nearly nine o'clock on the Ides of March. The act ends in a pervasive mood of foreboding.

The foreboding is carried immediately into the beginning of Act III, which opens with a flourish of trumpets as Caesar, accompanied by Brutus and the other conspirators, comes on to the stage.

> *Caesar* The ides of March are come.
> *Soothsayer* Ay, Caesar, but not gone.

People press around the great man urging petitions on him as he passes through the street. Artemidorus presses him to read what we know is his warning, on the grounds that 'that touches Caesar nearer', but Caesar replies with self-conscious nobility, 'What touches us ourself shall be last served.' It is a regal answer, using the royal 'we'. They all move on to the

Capitol. A remark made by Popilius Lena leads Cassius to believe that their plot is discovered, and he falls into a momentary fit of panic and despair:

> Brutus, what shall be done? If this be known,
> Cassius or Caesar never shall turn back,
> For I will slay myself.

It is interesting that it is the politic Cassius whose morale thus temporarily collapses. He tries to maintain the Stoic rhetoric of an earlier speech to Casca in 'Cassius or Caesar never shall turn back' but collapses into a despairing first-person with 'For I will slay myself'. It is Brutus, whom Cassius had earlier regarded as his instrument, who now takes control, and reassures Cassius.

The conspirators crowd round Caesar with petitions for the recall from exile of Publius Cimber. Caesar replies loftily, referring to himself in the third person, that he will not be moved from his original resolution. He concludes his first speech with

> Know, Caesar doth not wrong, nor without cause
> Will he be satisfied.

The last part of this sentence is curiously tame, if indeed it means anything at all. Ben Jonson complained in his *Timber, or Discoveries* that Shakespeare had written

> Caesar never did wrong, but with just cause,

and it is probable that this is what Shakespeare originally wrote, following it with the second line.

> Nor without cause will he be satisfied.

If this was Shakespeare's original version of the two lines, altered in deference to Ben Jonson's criticism, it can be argued that he was wrong to change it. For the lack of logic mocked by Jonson ('never did wrong, but with just cause') may be construed as precisely the grandiose kind of speech—asserting that what Caesar does, even if it is wrong on any vulgar standard, is by definition just—that might be expected from a powerful leader who considers himself a man of destiny. It would help to build up the image of the overweening, supremely confident dictator that is so suddenly destroyed by the actual murder.

his private conscience, can make something noble of a bloody murder. Antony asks permission to speak over Caesar's body in the market place, and Brutus readily agrees, to Cassius's consternation. Brutus brushes aside Cassius's alarmed protest that to allow Antony to speak at Caesar's funeral would be highly dangerous. Isn't he, Brutus, going to speak first, explaining his high reasons for the murder? And won't that make everything all right? Cassius is far from reassured, but Brutus wins, and Antony is allowed to speak over the body. For a moment Antony is left alone with the corpse on the stage to reveal his real feelings in a speech full of grief, bitterness and prophecy of direct revenge. The scene ends with Antony sending a message to Octavius Caesar to stay away from Rome in the present confusion and then announcing that he is going to try and work the people up in a speech.

At this stage the moral balance of the play is not clear. We have admired the gentleness, the nobility, the idealism, of Brutus, and seen how much he is respected in Rome; we have also seen his lack of self-knowledge, his tendency to confuse the issue by large abstractions and histrionic gestures, and his political naïveté. We have no great admiration for any of the other conspirators, all of whom seem to lack Brutus's idealism (for what that idealism is worth). We have seen Caesar as both a proud dictator and as a frail and fallible man, and Shakespeare has not emphasized one side more than the other. It is Antony who has all our attention now. His grief at Caesar's death is presented as something morally admirable. At the same time he has already revealed to the audience (and in a less degree to Cassius, though not at all to Brutus) the ambiguities of his position and his high skill in the deployment of expressions of feeling. The audience also now knows of his intention to try the feeling of the people. There seems to be a level of political sophistication here far beyond the ken of Brutus and even beyond the self-interested pragmatism of Cassius. And his language, in its concreteness and in the human appeal of its cadences, makes Brutus sound like an abstract logic-chopper and Cassius like a run-of-the-mill politician. We await in high suspense Brutus's public justification of the murder and, to an even greater degree, Antony's behaviour when he will be left alone with Caesar's body and the crowd.

There follows the famous scene where first Brutus then Antony address the crowd. There is always a problem in assessing within a play a set piece of rhetoric addressed by one of the characters to other characters. The audience of the play is also the audience of the rhetoric. Is the audience supposed to be moved in the same way as the characters on the stage to whom the piece is addressed? Or is the audience supposed to judge objectively the effect of the speech on the stage auditors? And does the audience also judge the quality of the speech and the degree to which it reflects the speaker's character? A massive piece of rhetoric on the stage is an extreme case of any speech on the stage, for all such speeches are addressed simultaneously to another stage character or characters and to the audience. The audience reacts partly as the recipient of the speech and partly as the observer of its meaning and effect in the wider context of the movement of meaning within the play. So Brutus's speech to the Roman crowd in the Forum is partly directed to us, the audience, by Shakespeare, and partly directed by one character created by Shakespeare to other characters he created. The same is true of Antony's speeches. But whereas the stage auditors of the speeches are involved only in their immediate response, the audience, being observers of the action rather than participators in it and having already had their interest in the character, motives and purposes of Brutus and Antony stimulated by previous scenes, are bound to respond in a complex way. If we are to be carried into a play at all and allow ourselves to respond adequately to its unfolding meaning, we must allow ourselves to be moved, and moved not only *by* the situation but, as it were, *within* the situation, letting the words of the characters create within us the responses of the stage characters who hear those words. Yet at the same time part of us must remain aloof, watching, judging, not only sensing how Brutus feels when moved by Antony but also noting the whole relationship between Antony and Brutus that the speech and its reception suggest and the place of that relationship in the total meaning of the play.

The situation is simpler with Brutus's speech than with Antony's. The former is brisk, logical, and abstract, apparently sincere yet oddly artificial. It is in carefully balanced prose, and the propositions it advances are almost geometrical in their ordered neatness. 'Not that I loved Caesar less, but that I loved Rome more. . . . As Caesar loved me, I weep for him; as he was fortunate, I rejoice at it; as he was valiant, I honour him; but as he was ambitious, I slew him. There is tears for his love; joy for his fortune; honour for his valour; and death for his ambition.' This does not seem to be intended as an example of bad rhetoric to be seen as such by the audience. It is effective in its way. But in its chopping up of a human individual into wholly separate aspects, which deserve respectively love, joy, honour and death, the speech reveals (to us if not to the crowd on stage) a certain desperation in the speaker's search for a motive for his action in murdering Caesar. To weep for the death of a man you love and rejoice when he is fortunate yet at the same time to kill him because he is ambitious is to apply to a human situation a kind of abstract logic that does violence to the realities of human existence and human relationships. You cannot, in fact, rejoice in a man's good fortune if that good fortune consists of military and political victory of a kind that produces the threat of tyranny that leads you to kill that man. You cannot say: 'As your friend I rejoice in your good fortune in becoming a dictator, but since dictatorship is a bad thing I must kill you for it.' The more we reflect on Brutus's speech the more we see that its balance and structure conceal an inner lack of logic. And it is interesting that the crowd, who are persuaded by the speech of Brutus's good intentions and of his nobility of character, have no idea of the nub of his argument, which is against too concentrated personal power. In their enthusiasm they would be happy to yield to Brutus the honours that Brutus has helped to kill Caesar for achieving. One of the crowd actually calls out, 'Let him be Caesar', thus making absolutely clear that Brutus, whose rhetoric has been disguised as logic, has aroused the crowd's emotions in his favour without conveying any idea at all of his motives and meaning. In other words, Brutus, the noble, rational idealist using what he believes to be straightforward logic in his address to the crowd, moves them to a state of wholly irrational approval of him personally. They don't know why they approve of him, but they do. And they are totally confused about what suitable action they should take to indicate their approval. Further, Brutus has no idea of what that action should be either. All he can think of saying to the crowd is that, when he leaves (as he does), they should stay and listen to Antony, who speaks at Caesar's funeral with the express permission of the conspirators.

With Brutus gone, Antony goes into the pulpit to face a suspicious crowd determined to hear no ill of Brutus. It is clear from the beginning, however, that Antony is a much more sophisticated manipulator of people than Brutus. The question of the audience's or reader's response to his rhetoric is more complex that it was with Brutus's speech, for the latter was short and its qualities easily discernible. Antony's speech, in carefully cadenced verse rather than Euclidian prose, moves in a series of sections, separated from each other by the responses of the stage auditors, which get progressively more favourable. But the audience's reaction moves in the reverse direction. We are first genuinely moved by Antony's words, we respect his emotion, we concede the doubt he voices as to whether Caesar really was ambitious as Brutus had said. But as he goes on the subsequent sections of his speech—particularly the blatant play with Caesar's will, saying that he could not possibly reveal it to them since if they were to know that they, the common people of Rome, were Caesar's heirs they would run riot (thus while protesting that he can't tell them he does tell them, and they *do* run riot, as he all along intended)—show him as a skilled and unscrupulous manipulator of others' feelings for his own purposes. We begin (and it is reasonable to believe that that is how Shakespeare planned the structure of the scene) by being one with the stage auditors and progressively detach ourselves from them to become interested in the totality of the action, in the struggle between Brutus and his group and Antony and his group, in the difference between the characters of Brutus and Antony, in the relation between language and character, and (if this is not to put it too grandiosely) in the complex relation between psychology, morality and politics.

It is interesting that the external patterning of the first part of Antony's speech is strictly logical, in some ways more so than Brutus's. It is true that the opening observation that men's evil deeds are remembered and their good deeds forgotten, 'so let it be with Caesar', is neither true nor logical, and represents a cautious, indeed rather fumbling, entry into his task of stirring up the crowd against the conspirators. He has to feel his way. But he soon moves into a logical structure. The noble Brutus told you Caesar was ambitious. *If* it were so, it was a grievous fault and grievously hath Caesar answered it. I am speaking by Brutus's leave, *For* Brutus is an honourable man. Caesar was faithful and just to me, *But* Brutus says he was ambitious, *And* Brutus is an honourable man. Caesar wept for the suffering poor. *Yet* Brutus said he was ambitious. *And* Brutus is an honourable man. Caesar thrice refused the crown, which didn't look like ambition. *Yet* Brutus says he was ambitious. I am not here to disprove what Brutus said, *But* here I am to speak what I do know. And with that line of beating monosyllables

> But here I am to speak what I do know

the balancing of 'ands' and 'buts', the apparently reasonable form of 'on the one hand' and 'on the other hand' comes to an end, and a frankly emotional tone takes over:

O judgement, thou art fled to brutish beasts,
And men have lost their reason. Bear with me.
My heart is in the coffin there with Caesar,
And I must pause till it come back to me.

It is ironical that just after the point at which he has abandoned reason to appeal to pure emotion, one of the crowd says, 'Methinks there is much reason in his sayings.' Nevertheless, members of the crowd have followed Antony's logic quite accurately.

Marked ye his words? He would not take the crown,
Therefore 'tis certain he was not ambitious.

Is this any stupider than Brutus's conviction that if he had been offered it yet again he might have accepted it, and that if he had his character would then have changed? But the main impact of Antony's speech on the crowd is emotional rather than logical, and his presentation of himself, at the end of the first part of his speech, as a man lost in uncontrollable grief, has its effect:

Poor soul! his eyes are red as fire with weeping.
There's not a nobler man in Rome than Antony.

With this reaction as testimony to his having found the right road, Antony continues going on to the patent trickery about the will and finally making it abundantly clear that with each repetition of the phrase 'honourable man' the ironic intention comes nearer to destroying the earlier pretence at logical balance, until with his sentence

I fear I wrong the honourable men
Whose daggers have stabbed Caesar: I do fear it,

he goads the crowd into shouting 'They were traitors. Honourable men!' And 'They were villains, murderers!' By this time our response to Antony's rhetoric has taken the form of admiration for his cunning, disapproval of his unscrupulousness, and wonder about what he is going to say next. He pretends to have forgotten about the will, and the crowd insists on his reading it. But he is not ready yet. He descends to the body and in a slow-moving elegiac speech produces a rhetoric that is the absolute contrary of the abstract logic-balancing that Brutus had engaged in:

If you have tears, prepare to shed them now.
You all do know this mantle; I remember
The first time ever Caesar put it on.
'Twas on a summer's evening in his tent,
That day he overcame the Nervii.

Here I think the theatre audience or reader takes a more wary view of what is said, seductive though the language is, than the stage auditors do. The specificness of the mantle, of the precise occasion when he first wore it, of the summer evening, the tent, the battle against the Nervii, is very appealing, and the crowd are clearly too moved to ask sceptically such questions as 'Do you really know the mantle? Do you really remember the first time ever Caesar put it on? Was it really a summer evening?' And when he goes further and professes to identify the precise rents made by Cassius's dagger and Casca's dagger and Brutus's dagger, we cannot but be aware of the absurdity of the pretended identification, though appreciating the appeal of such language to Antony's auditors. It is by setting the stage so precisely in time, place and detail, in language of poignantly elegiac tone, that Antony reaches the point where he can confidently brand Brutus first with ingratitude and then with treason. The elegy and the denunciation flow from each other:

Then I, and you, and all of us fell down,
While bloody treason flourished over us.
O now you weep, and I perceive you feel
The dint of pity. These are gracious drops.
Kind souls, what weep you when you but behold
Our Caesar's vesture wounded? Look you here,
Here is himself, marred as you see with traitors.

He pauses on that strong denunciatory word 'traitors' to let the crowd express their sorrow and indignation. He has now got them where he wants them. 'Revenge! About! Seek! Burn! Fire! Kill! Slay! Let not a traitor live.' But, either because he is carried away by his own virtuosity or because he wants to make assurance doubly sure, or perhaps for both reasons, he moves into another style of rhetoric. He talks more in sorrow than in anger of the 'private griefs' that must have led the 'honourable men' to behave as they did, thus simultaneously destroying at a blow Brutus's claim to have done the deed for public patriotic motives and

Brutus joins the petitioners, followed by Cassius, and this provokes Caesar to an even more grandiose statement of his fixity of purpose ('I am constant as the northern star'). Cinna then adds his voice, and Caesar dismisses him with

> Hence! Wilt thou lift up Olympus?

—an expression which represents the apex of the monument to himself that Caesar has been verbally building. But it is followed—and these are his last words except for the famous *Et tu, Brute* when Brutus delivers his stroke—by the more human and, in the circumstances, tragically ironic

> Doth not Brutus bootless kneel?

(I haven't even conceded this to Brutus, my dearest friend of all, so what hope is there that I shall give in to any of you others?) Then Casca stabs first, followed by the others, with Brutus last, and Caesar lies dead on the stage.

There is no pause. The successful conspirators immediately begin to shout slogans ('Liberty, freedom, and enfranchisement!'), while Brutus takes control. It is Brutus who reassures the old and infirm Publius—too feeble to flee—that no harm is intended to him or anybody else, and who assumes responsibility on behalf of the group. But in fact, now that the deed is done, Brutus is shown as being uncertain about his attitude. He nervously elaborates on a feeble jest by Casca to the effect that 'he who cuts off twenty years of life cuts off so many years of fearing death', as though that was his reason for joining the conspiracy. Then, in a self-consciously theatrical gesture, he tries to make a high ritual out of the gory business of murder by suggesting that they all bathe their hands in Caesar's blood up to the elbows and then proclaim their slogans throughout the streets as they wave their bloody arms. Leo Kirschbaum, in his essay 'Shakespeare's Stage Blood and Its Critical Significance',[1] points out the dramatic effect of Brutus's taking the lead in this savage ritual. 'However they may disagree on particulars, all commentators on Shakespeare's play regard Brutus as a man who does not understand himself or others. That the dignified and gentle Brutus should propose the ghastly procedure of the conspirators bathing their hands in the blood of Caesar's body wrenches the mind. It emphasizes the disorder in the man.' When Cassius suggests that Caesar's murder will be re-enacted

[1] *Proceedings of the Modern Language Association*, LXIV (1949), pp. 517–24.

many times in future generations, Brutus eagerly elaborates the point, as though seeking to turn a horrible physical reality into ritual drama. On Shakespeare's stage the goriness of the scene was visually emphasized in the most realistic way (we have abundant evidence for this): for someone involved in such a scene to start chatting about future play-acting is incongruous, and the incongruity makes a dramatic point.

Then Antony's servant arrives, and in repeating *verbatim* the message his master had given him to deliver introduces a new kind of rhetoric into this rhetorical play:

> Brutus is noble, wise, valiant, and honest;
> Caesar was mighty, bold, royal, and loving.
> Say I love Brutus and I honour him;
> Say I feared Caesar, honoured him, and loved him. . . .

As the speech continues, with its cunning balancing of phrases, its matching of flattery of Brutus with praise of the dead Caesar, its offer to join his fortunes to Brutus if Brutus can convince him that Caesar really deserved to die, we are aware of the voice of the skilled manipulator, the voice of Antony, who, unlike Brutus, knows both himself and others and, unlike Cassius, knows how to conceal his feelings and bide his time. Brutus, a simpleton beside the subtle Antony, takes the speech at its face value, and replies courteously and reassuringly. 'I know that we shall have him well to friend,' he says to Cassius of Antony, but Cassius is less certain: 'I wish we may. But yet I have a mind / That fears him much. . . .' Not for the first time, Brutus is wrong and Cassius right about Antony, but Brutus's advice is followed.

The entry of Antony's servant—it is in a sense an entry of Antony himself, for it is Antony's very words that the servant repeats to Brutus—has been seen by several critics as the turning point of the play. The first movement had been the persuasion of Brutus to join the conspiracy, its planning and its execution. Now the counter-movement starts. In a sense it starts the moment the murder is accomplished and the principal conspirators fall to sloganizing, gesturing and play-acting. They don't really know what to do now. They have put an end to Caesar's power but are unable to put any new power in its place, and so, as it soon emerges, they have unleashed the worst kind of chaos, civil war, which can only be put to an end by a reassertion, on a much less humanly sympathetic level, of the very 'spirit of Caesar' that Brutus thought the murder of Caesar would destroy. It is Antony who makes sure (for his own reasons) that this will indeed be the consequences of the murder.

The entry of Antony himself is followed at once by his grief-stricken address to Caesar's body. Antony is a manipulator and accomplished role-taker, but the speech he makes here begins in genuine grief; its cadences, the placing of the pauses, the tone of voice, all suggest spontaneity. But when he turns from addressing the body to addressing the conspirators the tone is cool and carefully calculated:

> I know not, gentlemen, what you intend,
> Who else must be let blood, who else is rank.
> If I myself, there is no hour so fit
> As Caesar's death hour; nor no instrument
> Of half that worth as those your swords, made rich
> With the most noble blood of all this world. . . .

He could never die so fittingly

> As here by Caesar, and by you cut off,
> The choice and master spirits of this age.

He is taking a calculated risk (is that last line ironical, and will it be taken as such?); but he knows his Brutus, who exclaims in genuine shock, 'O Antony, beg not your death of us!' The conspirators, Brutus urges, did what they did not out of blood lust or cruelty but in 'pity to the general wrong of Rome' (a typical Brutus abstraction). For Antony they have nothing but 'kind love, good thoughts, and reverence'. But, as Cassius knows and as Cassius knows that Antony knows, kind words butter no parsnips. Cassius has listened uneasily first to Antony, then to Brutus, and he chips in with his own more realistic offer to Antony:

> Your voice shall be as strong as any man's
> In the disposing of new dignities.

He at least knows what it is all about—power—even though his moral domination by Brutus will prevent him ever acting effectively on that knowledge.

Brutus now intervenes with another characteristic remark (' . . . I, that did love Caesar when I struck him . . .'), to which Antony replies in a tone at once cool and ambiguous, 'I doubt not of your wisdom.' Then he, too, almost as though he were mocking Brutus's tendency to engage in ritual gestures, takes the bloody hands of the conspirators one by one in a histrionic gesture of friendship. There is something strange and sinister—to the audience, and perhaps to Cassius, if not to Brutus—in the solemn shaking of the murderers' bloody hands by the murdered man's close friend. When finally he turns to Trebonius ('Though last, not least in love, yours, good Trebonius'), the very man who had taken him aside so that the murderers could have a clear run, to greet him in terms of apparent love and admiration, the whole play becomes momentarily focussed on Antony and the ambiguity of his position poises the action in doubt and uneasy expectation. He goes on to admit his predicament, with a break in the movement of his speech that is at the same time rhetorically effective and genuinely revealing:

> Gentlemen all—Alas, what shall I say?
> My credit now stands on such slippery ground
> That one of two bad ways you must conceit me,
> Either a coward or a flatterer.

He goes on to talk with feeling of the dead Caesar, the rhetoric of grief replacing the rhetoric of politics, and again we feel both that the grief is genuine and that he is taking a calculated risk in voicing it at this time in this company in this way.

> Pardon me, Julius! Here wast thou bayed, brave hart;
> Here didst thou fall; and here thy hunters stand,
> Signed in thy spoil and crimsoned in thy lethe . . .

Brutus had said that the murder of Caesar would be a sacrifice, but Antony sees the dead Caesar not as a sacrifice but as a brave stag slaughtered in the chase. Cassius nervously interrupts Antony's praise of Caesar, and when Antony explains that that is the least he can say in the circumstances Cassius brushes the matter aside with the cold practical question, 'But what compact mean you to have with us?' 'Friends am I with you all and love you all,'' he replies (not answering Cassius's question, but almost echoing Brutus in his protestation of love for those he is bound to oppose)—provided 'that you shall give me reason / Why and wherein Caesar was dangerous.' 'Or else were this a savage spectacle,' replies Brutus, confident once more that his moral intentions, is very ready to insist on the seriousness of his own character, especially in contrast with that of Antony:

> I am not gamesome. I do lack some part
> Of that quick spirit that is Antony.

Cassius welcomes the introduction of the subject of Brutus's character, and it does not take him long before he has Brutus confessing his inward perplexity:

> Vexed I am
> Of late with passions of some difference [i.e., conflicting emotions],
> Conceptions only proper to myself, . . .

Only proper to himself? If they had remained so, there would have been no tragedy. As we shall see, one of Brutus's problems was that he could not easily distinguish between passions proper to himself and those relevant to a public situation. Even when he talks about himself in a tone of self-pity he is capable of talking of himself in the third person (as Caesar does, for different reasons). His friends must not be grieved

> Nor construe any further my neglect
> Than that poor Brutus, with himself at War,
> Forgets the show of love to other men.

The slow, plangent tone of these lines is very much in the Brutus idiom. It is part of his charm (as what Wilson Knight called the 'Othello music' is part of the charm of Othello when he is truly himself): there is a concerned brooding sadness in many of his speeches, when he talks to his wife or to his servant Lucius as well as when he talks to and of himself. Cassius does not give him time to develop this tone. He intervenes to suggest that Brutus cannot really see himself as others see him: he does not appreciate his own 'hidden worthiness' nor is he aware that

> many of the best respect in Rome
> (Except immortal Caesar), speaking of Brutus
> And groaning underneath this age's yoke,
> Had wished that noble Brutus had his eyes.

Now it is out: Cassius wants Brutus to share his view of 'this age's yoke'. Brutus is startled to hear the matter put so bluntly and, in a quite different tone of voice, asks

> Into what dangers would you lead me, Cassius,
> That you would have me seek into myself
> For that which is not in me?

But it *is* in him, as Cassius undertakes to show. He is interrupted by a 'flourish and shout', and Brutus reacts as Cassius wants him to:

> What means this shouting? I do fear the people
> Choose Caesar for their king.

Cassius pounces on that word 'fear' in order to force Brutus to admit that he 'would not have it so'.

So far, we have been shown little of the character and motives of Cassius, except indirectly. We have the remarkable spectacle of Cassius persuading Brutus to join in some kind of movement against Caesar without Cassius himself saying what he thinks of the matter at all. He professes to be merely holding a mirror up to Brutus and showing him the Brutus that other people see. By this method he has got Brutus to admit that he would not wish to see Caesar king, 'yet I love him well'. He has also got him to mount his high moral-rhetorical horse and ride on it towards the goal that Cassius wants him to reach:

> What is it that you would impart to me?
> If it be aught toward the general good,
> Set honour in one eye and death i' th' other,
> And I will look on both indifferently;
> For let the gods so speed me as I love
> The name of honour more than I fear death.

He is talking about himself, and in highly abstract terms. He loves 'the name of honour' more than he fears death. This is the language of public rhetoric, not of inward debate. Now we must not be too censorious about this. We know that it was an accepted convention of Shakespeare's stage that characters can talk of their own virtue in a purely informative way, without being accused of egotism. Nevertheless, Brutus's sliding away from the particular question of the state of Rome to talk about honour and death is characteristic of him. This is part of his 'nobility'. He is shown in the play as possessing a theoretical and abstract mind in dealing with moral and political questions, as the extraordinary abstractness of his inward argument in favour of murdering Caesar (II, i, 10 ff.) demonstrates conclusively; yet he can be warmly human in dealing directly with individuals, especially in situations that have a dash of melancholy in them. His two modes are the rhetorical and the elegiac. How different is Cassius's mode, as appears in the speech with which he replies to Brutus's talk of honour and death. Yes, he virtually says, I'm glad you said that, for 'honour is the subject of my story'. But is it? He goes on to express, in excited, irascible verse, his outrage that a man like Caesar, whom he once had to rescue from the flooded Tiber after Caesar had challenged him to join in swimming across it, should have grown so much more powerful than himself. The thought makes him splutter with anger. He goes on to describe how he once saw Caesar shaking with fever in Spain. ''Tis true, this god did shake.' Though he has already said that the shaking was due to fever, he goes on, in irrational anger, to ascribe it to cowardice: 'His coward lips did from their colour fly.' And in his high fever Caesar had to ask Titinius for a drink 'as a sick girl'. He is almost stuttering with rage. Honour is not the subject of his story at all: he is raging with jealousy:

> Ye gods, it doth amaze me
> A man of such a feeble temper should
> So get the start of the majestic world
> And bear the palm alone.

He is interrupted by another shout and flourish, which lead Brutus to express the fear that some new honours 'are heaped on Caesar' and provoke Cassius to an even stronger outburst. He tries to get Brutus to share his outrage at the *disparity* between Caesar's present position and their own.

> 'Brutus' and 'Caesar'. What should be in that 'Caesar'?
> Why should that name be sounded more than yours?

He goes on to compare the two *names*, concluding that one is as good as the other. This is the expression of something more than jealousy: there is a sense of absolute outrage that one man should so tower over others of the same class, and a kind of genuine egalitarian passion sounding through his language (egalitarian, that is, within the limits of a single social class). There is no suggestion that Brutus is especially touched by this kind of argument (the actor playing Brutus should perhaps look at Cassius with slight puzzlement during this part of his speech), but, perhaps sensing this, Cassius then hits on a point that he knows will come forcibly home to Brutus:

> O, you and I have heard our fathers say
> There was a Brutus once that would have brooked
> Th'eternal devil to keep his state in Rome
> As easily as a king.

'King' was the ultimate bad word for Brutus, whose ancestor Lucius Junius Brutus, as he himself boasts in II, i, 53–4, 'did from the streets of Rome / The Tarquin drive when he was called a king'. The reference to Brutus's ancestor expelling Tarquin and so founding the Roman Republic has more effect than the comparisons of names or the anger at Caesar's greatness. Brutus now replies soberly and at first in a private voice, that he is aware what Cassius is getting at and will think about it. But he cannot stay in the private mode long in dealing with such a subject, and he ends his speech with another rhetorical reference to himself in the third person:

> Brutus had rather be a villager
> Than to repute himself a son of Rome
> Under these hard conditions as this time
> Is like to lay upon us.

Caesar and his train now return, with Caesar looking angry, Calphurnia pale, 'and all the rest look like a chidden train'. We hear Caesar talking to Antony, complaining of Cassius's 'lean and hungry look' and of his thinking too much. 'Fear him not, Caesar,' says Antony, and Caesar replies:

> Would he were fatter! But I fear him not.
> Yet if my name were liable to fear,
> I do not know the man I should avoid
> So soon as that same Cassius.

Here Shakespeare is deliberately, perhaps even playfully, setting side by side the human Caesar and Caesar the role-taking dictator. He goes on to dwell on Cassius's ironic and ascetic character, so unlike Antony:

establishing his own generosity of feeling. His picture of himself as the 'plain blunt man' contrasted with the oratorically skilled Brutus is an old rhetorical trick, and though it cannot fool the theatre audience or the reader it certainly fools the crowd. The appeal to Caesar's wounds 'poor poor dumb mouths' to speak for him, and the outrageous assertion that

> were I Brutus
> And Brutus Antony, there were an Antony
> Would ruffle up your spirits, and put a tongue
> In every wound of Caesar that should move
> The stones of Rome to rise and mutiny

enable him to persuade the crowd that he has not played any rhetorical tricks on them in the very act of playing such tricks, and also to end on the strongly provocative word 'mutiny'.

We now get the ironical touch (ironical to us, but, it must be insisted again, not to Antony's stage auditors: the difference in reaction is part of the play's meaning) that, the crowd having in their excitement forgotten about the will, Antony, who had shortly before insisted that he could not possibly read it, reminds them of it and proceeds to read it. The resulting proof of Caesar's generosity to the common people completes Antony's case and provides the final fuel for the righteous indignation of the crowd. They disperse to set fire to the conspirators houses and to 'pluck down benches. Pluck down forms, windows, anything!' Antony, left alone, relishes the coming riot:

> Now let it work. Mischief, thou art afoot,
> Take thou what course thou wilt.

A servant enters and tells him that Octavius has arrived in Rome and that Brutus and Cassius have fled the city. 'Fortune is merry, / And in this mood will give us anything,' comments Antony on the first piece of news and on the second remarks complacently:

> Belike they had some notice of the people,
> How I had moved them.

This is the virtuoso taking pride in the effects of his own skill. The cunning orator, the manipulator of crowds, now turns to the practical ends to which his oratory was a means. 'Bring me to Octavius,' he says to the servant and they both leave the stage.

Act III ends with the short scene in which Cinna the poet is torn to pieces by the crowd because, although he was not one of the conspirators and was a friend of Caesar's, he bears a name identical to that of Cinna the conspirator. This is not only a vividly sinister example of the murderous irrationality of an enflamed crowd on the loose, the direct result of Antony's oratory. It is also, if less directly, a critical parody of the logic which Brutus used to persuade himself and then others of the need to murder Caesar. A member of the crowd, after hearing Cinna protest that he is Cinna the poet and not Cinna the conspirator, shouts: 'It is no matter; his name's Cinna! Pluck but his name out of his heart, and turn him going.' So Brutus had wanted to be able to kill Caesar's spirit without dismembering Caesar, but, finding this impossible, decided to kill his body in order to destroy his spirit.

Act IV opens with Antony, Octavius and Lepidus, joint inheritors of the spirit of Caesar and leaders of the battle against Brutus, Cassius and the other conspirators, plotting together about power. It is an ugly scene: the three are coolly deciding on the list of people to be got rid of. There is no pretence that anything is at stake except naked power.

Octavius Your brother too must die. Consent you Lepidus?
Lepidus I do consent.
Octavius Prick him down Antony.
Lepidus Upon condition Publius shall not live,
Who is your sister's son, Mark Antony.
Antony He shall not live. Look, with a spot I damn him.

When Lepidus leaves and Octavius and Antony are left alone to talk together Antony makes absolutely clear his contempt for the third member of the triumvirate. He is 'a slight, unmeritable man, meet to be sent on errands', unfit to share their threefold rule. In the ensuing conversation Antony is the dominating figure, emphasizing his greater age and experience and tossing aside Octavius's defence of Lepidus that 'he's a tried and valiant soldier' by replying, 'So is my horse, Octavius.' Lepidus is someone to be used and then cast aside. 'Do not talk of him / But as a property.' Far from trying to explain their actions and motives as Brutus always explained his, in terms of abstract ideals and public idealism, Antony and Octavius talk the language of *Realpolitik*. Brutus, we feel at this stage, may be a self-deceiver who lacks full understanding both of his own motives and those of others, but if the alternative is this cold-blooded jostling for power, it is not shown as in any way preferable. It is clear enough by now that *Julius Caesar* is not a morality play about either the superiority of public idealism to power politics or the superiority of political realism to well-meaning but self-deceiving idealism. There is no simple correlation between morality and effective public order.

The next scene opens with hints of a breach between Brutus and Cassius conveyed in a conversation between Brutus and Lucilius. Then 'Enter Cassius and his Powers' and the nature of the breach is made evident. The stage direction reminds us that we are in a military camp. The first encounter between Brutus and Cassius is in terms of military discipline:

Cassius Stand ho!
Brutus Stand ho! Pass the word along.
1st Soldier Stand!
2nd Soldier Stand!
3rd Soldier Stand!

Then, in a cadence we have not yet heard in the play, Cassius speaks:

Cassius Most noble brother, you have done me wrong.
Brutus Judge me, you gods! wrong I mine enemies?
And if not so, how should I wrong a brother.

Cassius's tone, surprisingly perhaps, is the more dignified and generous. Brutus is simply self-righteous, answering Cassius's courteous reproach with a rhetorical question and an abstract piece of logic. But Brutus at least realizes that the two leaders should not quarrel before their men, so the scene moves at once to Brutus's tent where the two quarrel privately. The quarrel scene is one of the most famous in Shakespeare and has been much written about. Brutus appears in it as the moral man, Cassius as the practical, realistic man, yet in a sense Cassius emerges as the more attractive character, even morally. Brutus is indignant that Cassius has not punished people for taking bribes and he also accuses Cassius of selling offices for gold. Brutus is outraged that, having killed 'great Julius . . . for justice sake' one of them should be besmirching the high cause by taking bribes. As he reproaches Cassius, his language soars: this is not the Brutus of the conversation with Portia or the considerate words for the boy Lucius (though we are to hear that Brutus again soon): it is a Brutus who addresses Cassius like a public meeting and as a conscious representative of public morality. They are in the middle of a dangerous civil war, and Cassius is genuinely taken aback by Brutus's attitude:

> You forget yourself
> To hedge me in. I am a soldier, I,
> Older in practice, abler than yourself
> To make conditions.

With his profession of superiority in military experience Cassius provokes Brutus into dropping his high moral language and adopting the simple language of a squabbling schoolboy. For a moment the whole scene degenerates into this:

> *Brutus* Go to! You are not, Cassius.
> *Cassius* I am.
> *Brutus* I say you are not.

But it is Brutus who turns the dialogue into a slanging match, with his 'Away, slight man!' and 'Shall I be frighted when a madman stares?' This is a tone we have never heard from Brutus before:

> Go show your slaves how choleric you are
> And make your bondmen tremble. Must I budge?
> Must I observe you? Must I stand and crouch
> Under your testy humour? By the gods,
> You shall digest the venom of your spleen,
> Though it do split you: for from this day forth
> I'll use you for my mirth, yea, for my laughter,
> When you are waspish.

Yet it is Brutus, not Cassius, who shows spleen in this scene. Cassius never becomes enraged. He is in turn reproachful, avuncular, admonishing, incredulous, placatory. Indeed, the shifts in Cassius's tone, which control the quarrel and finally enable it to be resolved, determine the movement and structure of the whole scene. When Brutus goes on to taunt Cassius with having boasted of being a better soldier, Cassius tries to turn away his anger:

> You wrong me in every way! You wrong me, Brutus!
> I said an elder soldier, not a better.
> Did I say 'better'?

There is something so human and natural and even engaging in this pleading attempt to stop the quarrel that from this moment Cassius—self-interested though we know he was in planning Caesar's murder—takes on a new character or rather, our previous knowledge of his character is enriched and subtilized with new touches that make him more convincing and more attractive.

Brutus is not yet ready for a reconciliation. When Cassius protests that he said elder soldier, not better soldier Brutus sullenly mutters, 'If you did, I care not.' This is too much for Cassius, who exclaims

> When Caesar lived he durst not thus have moved me.

To which Brutus replies, truly enough, that Cassius 'durst not so have tempted him'. But in fact Cassius has not 'tempted' (i.e. provoked) Brutus to anything like the degree that Brutus has provoked Cassius. Brutus goes on now to attack Cassius for not sending him 'certain sums of gold' he had asked. He refuses on moral grounds to raise money in the only practicable way in the circumstances and bitterly reproaches Cassius for doing so; yet he reproaches him equally bitterly for not sending him money that Cassius must have raised in the way Brutus so disapproves of. *I* can't raise money that way, he righteously proclaims:

> I did send to you
> For certain sums of gold, which you denied me;
> For I can raise no money by vile means.
> By heaven, I had rather coin my heart
> And drop my blood for drachmas than to wring
> From the hard hands of peasants their vile trash
> By any indirection.

The 'for' in the third line of this quotation makes it clear that the reason he asked Cassius to send him the money was because he could not bring himself, for moral reasons, to collect it the way Cassius had done. Yet the legions had to be paid, and Cassius was to blame for not sending him the money to pay them:

> I did send
> To you for gold to pay my legions,
> Which you denied me. Was that done like Cassius?
> Should I have answered Caius Cassius so?

When Marcus Brutus grows so covetous
To lock such rascal counters from his friends,
Be ready, gods, with all your thunderbolts,
Dash him to pieces!

He is off, talking about himself grandiloquently in the third person. At the same time the reproachful 'Was that done like Cassius?' sounds a more conciliatory note than his earlier outbursts. Cassius seizes on this, asserting that he did not deny Brutus the money and was misreported, going in to sound a tone of sad, reproachful friendliness which marks the real transition towards the reconciliation:

Brutus has rived my heart:
A friend should bear his friend's infirmities,
But Brutus makes mine greater than they are.

Brutus is still stiff. 'I do not like your faults,' he replies, and when Cassius says that a friendly eye would never see them, Brutus answers equally coldly that 'A flatterer's would not, though they do appear / As huge as high Olympus.' Cassius is trying hard, but he cannot move Brutus out of his sullen anger. So he tries a deliberate rhetorical outburst, crying out that he is hated by one he loves, that life is no longer worth living, and offering his dagger and his naked breast to Brutus:

Strike as thou didst at Caesar; for I know,
When thou didst hate him worst, thou lovedst him better
Than ever thou lovedst Cassius.

This at last breaks down Brutus's self-righteously angry mood. The rhythm of his speech changes to the slow sad cadence we have heard before in Brutus as he apologizes for his outburst of anger. The human feeling in this exchange completely obliterates the public issues with which the play opened and for which Brutus and Cassius are now waging war. Indeed, from this moment there is no real conviction in anything either of them say about public affairs. They both settle into a mood of personal sadness and political indifference. The language is movingly ordinary:

Brutus When I spoke that, I was ill-tempered too.
Cassius Do you confess so much? Give me your hand.
Brutus And my heart too.

Cassius O Brutus!
Brutus What's the matter?
Cassius Have you not love enough to bear with me
When that rash humour which my mother gave me
Makes me forgetful?

This is very engaging, and we accept it at its face value until we go back over the scene and realize that it is Brutus who has shown a 'rash humour', not Cassius. If we compare the tone of Brutus's and Cassius's speeches during the quarrel, we shall find that Brutus was by far the more violent, while Cassius kept seeking an entry for a more conciliatory manner. Brutus accepts Cassius's explanation with grave affection, without ever questioning the fact on which it is based. Somehow this is made to reflect credit on both characters: Cassius takes the blame in order to be certain of ending the quarrel and recementing their friendship, while Brutus, his anger burned out, no longer realizes which of them was the more angry and eagerly accepts the way back to affection proposed by Cassius. The effect of all this is to withdraw both Brutus and Cassius from the political dimension of the play, which is left now to the realism of the other side, whom we have already seen coldly deciding to have their friends and relations killed off for political reasons and for whom personal relationships are simply a means to power. And this helps to turn the total meaning of the play towards the paradox that effective political solutions to problems of power do not arise automatically from the most acceptable human relationships on the personal level.

The entry of a bad poet to chide the two generals for quarrelling, at the very moment when they have made up their quarrel (adapted from an incident described by Plutarch), shows Brutus dismissing the intruder with contempt while Cassius says, 'Bear with him, Brutus. 'Tis his fashion.' Again it is Cassius who shows the kindlier feeling. But when the two are left alone again and Brutus blurts out 'O Cassius, I am sick of many griefs' the spontaneous authenticity of the utterance wins us back to him. He now reveals that his wife Portia has committed suicide and this throws new light on his earlier behaviour, in spite of his self-conscious Stoicism ('No man bears sorrow better,' he says of himself) and his refusal to allow Cassius to dwell on the subject.

Speak no more of her. Give me a bowl of wine.
In this I bury all unkindness, Cassius.

Cassius says, 'I cannot drink too much of Brutus's love', and this is not a pretence of friendship for political ends. The human (as distinct from the political) dimension dominates their relationship.

The second introduction of the theme of Portia's death, received by Brutus as though he had not known it before, must surely be seen as a revision by Shakespeare to replace the earlier announcement which through inadvertence was left in the text, rather than a device to make out Brutus a hypocrite who pretended to be ignorant of something he already knew about in order to demonstrate how stoically he could take the news. It is followed by a difference of opinion between Brutus and Cassius—expressed in the gentlest and friendliest terms this time—as to whether they should march to Philippi and seek battle with the enemy there (Brutus's view) or whether, as Cassius urges, they should stay where they are and let the enemy wear themselves out in seeking them. We are made to feel, I think, that Cassius's view is the more realistic, but Brutus, confident in the superiority of his argument, brushes Cassius's points aside with cheerful confidence and Cassius, though he knows Brutus is wrong, cannot bring himself to break the new-found atmosphere of friendship by disagreeing further. So the fatal decision is taken in the name of friendship. They retire for the night with Cassius deferring to Brutus—'Good night, *my lord*'—and Brutus replying in a tone of brotherly affection—'Good night, *good brother*.'

Brutus is left alone with the boy Lucius, in speaking to whom he recovers those compassionately plangent domestic tones he had used in speaking to Portia in Act II scene 1. This is Brutus at his most attractive—and at his most real, for the public Brutus speaks in an artificial voice using a rhetoric that is almost dehumanized in its abstractness. When he finds his book in the pocket of his gown the humanizing touch is at its most appealing:

Brutus Look, Lucius, here's the book I sought for so;
I put it in the pocket of my gown.
Lucius I was sure your lordship did not give it me.
Brutus Bear with me good boy, I am much forgetful.
Canst thou hold up thy heavy eyes awhile,
And touch thy instrument a strain or two?
Lucius Ay, my lord, an't please you.
Brutus It does, my boy.
I trouble thee too much, but thou art willing.

Brutus sees that Lucius is almost asleep, and promises not to keep him long:

> I will not hold thee long. If I do live,
> I will be good to thee.

'Musicke, and a Song', says the Folio stage direction here. Lucius falls asleep as he plays and sings. In this hushed night-time atmosphere Brutus turns gently to the boy, bidding him good night. 'I will not do thee so much wrong to wake thee.' He then turns to his book:

> Let me see, let me see. Is not the leaf turned down
> Where I left reading? Here it is I think.

We need not worry about the anachronism that has Brutus turning down the leaf of his book (which would have been a scroll to unroll rather than a book to have its pages turned). The point is that the intense privacy of the scene is here emphasized most strongly. It is precisely at this point, when the private Brutus, the humane, considerate, scholarly Brutus, has started to read, that the Ghost of Caesar enters. In Plutarch's Life of Brutus the ghost is not identified as Caesar at all:

> So, being ready to go into Europe, one night very late, when all the camp took quiet rest, as he was in his tent with a little light, thinking of weighty matters, he thought he heard one come in to him and, casting his eye towards the door of his tent, that he saw a wonderful strange and monstrous shape of a body coming towards him, and said never a word. So Brutus boldly asked what he was, a god or a man, and what cause brought him thither. The spirit answered him:
>
> 'I am thy evil spirit, Brutus; and thou shalt see me by the city of Philippes.'
>
> Brutus, being no otherwise afraid, replied again unto it:
>
> 'Well, then I shall see thee again.'

Shakespeare constructs the whole scene with Lucius out of Plutarch's 'one night very late, when all the camp took quiet rest'. The ghost, identified as Caesar only in the stage direction, is seen by Brutus as 'this monstrous apparition' (echoing North's Plutarch); he identifies himself, as in Plutarch, as 'thy evil spirit, Brutus' and, again as in Plutarch, tells Brutus he shall see him at Philippi, to which Brutus replies simply, 'Why, I shall see thee at Philippi then.' The great difference between Shakespeare's treatment of the incident and the incident in Plutarch is that Shakespeare positions it so as to have Brutus's evil spirit, who is the spirit of Caesar he had earlier wished to destroy, intrude on him at his fullest moment of self-realizing privacy. In this context, the calm acceptance of the ghost's presence and prophecy is an indication of how far Brutus has removed himself from the rhetorically conceived public mission which led him to join Caesar's murderers. He discovers that neither Lucius nor Varro nor Claudius has seen the ghost: it is a private visitation of the spirit of a public figure. Brutus is not very interested. Only his own private self, which is his best self, is now real. But he has to carry on with his public role, though in a fatalistic spirit. Act IV ends with Brutus giving military orders:

> Go and commend me to my brother Cassius.
> Bid him set on his powers betimes before,
> And we will follow.

Act V opens with the immediate prospect of battle between the two sides. 'Enter Octavius, Antony, and their Army' says the Folio stage direction, and Octavius's speech makes it clear at once that Brutus's advice that they should move on to the plains of Philippi was (as Cassius knew even when he accepted it) playing into the enemy's hands. The confident Antony assures Octavius that 'I am in their bosoms' and knows precisely what Brutus and Cassius are thinking and will do. But just as we are prepared to see the subtle and politic Antony dominate his younger companion, Octavius suddenly, quietly, and effectively asserts his superiority. It is he, after all, who is Caesar's heir and nephew and it is he who will be the real beneficiary of a victory against the conspirators.

> *Antony* Octavius, lead your battle softly on
> Upon the left hand of the even field.
> *Octavius* Upon the right hand I. Keep you the left.
> *Antony* Why do you cross me in this exigent? [oppose me at this critical moment]
> *Octavius* I do not cross you: but I will do so.

There is no answering this calm assertion of power. From now on Antony is regarded by Octavius as more of a talker than a doer, even though (as Plutarch recorded and Shakespeare accepted) the wing of the army led by

Octavius was overthrown by Brutus while Antony defeated 'Cassius's legions'. According to Plutarch, Antony had all the credit for the victory over the conspirators at Philippi. 'Thus Antonius had the chiefest glory of all this victory, specially because Caesar [Octavius] was sick at that time.' Shakespeare rejects this, making no mention of Octavius's sickness: he needs him as the play moves into its concluding movement to represent the passionless man of effective political action, just as Antony represents the passionate man who, artful and cunning though he is, cannot in the end compete with his more bloodless rival (and finally, as Shakespeare shows in *Antony and Cleopatra*, meets what Granville-Barker called 'the nemesis of the sensual man').

The set debate between the leaders of the two opposing factions before the battle commences represents an old heraldic tradition. It gives Shakespeare the opportunity to bring his four chief characters together for the last time in such a way as to emphasize that this is a *civil* war: the opponents know each other and use their personal knowledge in exchanging insults. The words versus deeds contrast is made early in the debate:

Brutus Words before blows. Is it so, countrymen?
Octavius Not that we love words better, as you do.

Brutus's 'countrymen' rings out sadly: Shakespeare's audience was sensitive to the horrors of civil war, and to have it emphasized at this point that it is *countrymen* who are fighting each other adds to the tragic atmosphere of the scene. But there is also something petty and schoolboyish in the tone of the debate. 'Not that we love words better, as you do,' is childish repartee. It is Antony who raises the level of the talk above that of childish bickering with his passionate charge of hypocrisy against the conspirators:

Witness the hole you made in Caesar's heart,
Crying 'Love live! Hail, Caesar!'

When Cassius taunts Antony with being a talker and not a doer ('The posture of your blows are yet unknown; / But for your words, they rob the Hybla bees, and leave them honeyless') Antony is roused to a kind of passionate rhetoric different from any variety of rhetoric he has so far employed in the play:

Villains! You did not so when your vile daggers
Hacked one another in the sides of Caesar.
You showed your teeth like apes, and fawned like hounds,
And bowed like bondmen, kissing Caesar's feet,
Whilst damnèd Casca, like a cur, behind
Struck Caesar on the neck. O you flatterers!

This rhetoric is not posed: it is a genuine, spontaneous outburst. It provokes from Cassius an equally spontaneous reply, to the effect that if Brutus had taken his (Cassius's) advice, Antony would not now be alive to insult them in this way. The whole debate is breaking out of policy into simple anger, and it is the voice of the cool, controlled, passionless Octavius that recalls them to a realization of what they are there for:

Come, come, the cause! If arguing makes us sweat,
The proof of it will turn to redder drops.
Look,
I draw a sword against conspirators . . .

Octavius's drawing of his sword is not a theatrical gesture, like Antony's gesture in pointed to the rents in Caesar's toga when he spoke over his body in the Forum, nor is it a symbolic gesture of the kind Brutus indulged in when bathing his arms in the murdered Caesar's blood. It simply shows us the brisk man of action cutting through the fog of language with the promise of immediate deeds. In calling Brutus and Cassius traitors, he provokes a protest from Brutus, still convinced of the patriotic disinterestedness of his participation in Caesar's murder. Something of the complacent self-righteousness seen earlier in Brutus returns when he replies to Octavius's remark that he 'was not born to die on Brutus's sword',

O, if thou wert the noblest of thy strain,
Young man, thou couldst not die more honourable.

This is Brutus seeing himself as a public figure, not, as we have seen, the most attractive Brutus. It is followed by a flash of the true Cassius, for whom all quarrels are at bottom personal not public. He derides the two leaders of the enemy as

A peevish schoolboy, worthless of such honour,
Joined with a masker and a reveller.

Antony recognizes that this is the true Cassius speaking, with his 'Old Cassius still', where we almost hear a note of reluctant affection. Again, the emphasis is on the fact that these people all know each other well. The quarrel is rapidly returning to the more personal level, at which issues of high policy and political principle will be lost in mere anger, when Octavius steps in to stop it. 'Come, Antony. Away!' he cries, and leaves with Antony and the army to prepare for battle.

Octavius's sense of purpose is contrasted with the resigned fatalism displayed by Brutus and Cassius who are now left with companions on the stage. The very movement of the verse they speak slows down; the cadence is mournful, the tone foreboding. Cassius expresses his conviction that it was a mistake all along to 'set upon one battle all our liberties' and confesses that, although previously an Epicurean in philosophy who had no use for omens and portents, he is now inclined to believe in such things, and fears the worst. His language is that of a man who has already given up:

> If we lose this battle, then is this
> The very last time we shall speak together.
> What are you then determined to do?

In Brutus's reply to this question there is a confusion of public gesture and private feeling. First he tells Cassius that he disapproves of suicide and believes it to be cowardly to show distrust of providence by killing oneself. But when Cassius inquires if he would then be contented 'to be led in triumph / Through the streets of Rome' he says he would not, talking of himself in the third person almost for the last time:

> Think not, thou noble Roman,
> That ever Brutus will go bound to Rome.
> He bears too great a mind.

But he cannot sustain this public pose. They will soon know the end of the 'work the ides of March begun' and perhaps they will never meet again. So they had better say farewell to each other. The plangent personal note takes over:

> For ever and for ever farewell, Cassius!
> If we do meet again, why we shall smile;
> If not, why then this parting was well made.

Cassius takes up his part in the sorrowful duet:

> For ever and for ever farewell, Brutus!
> If we do meet again, we'll smile indeed;
> If not, 'tis true this parting was well made.

The scene ends with Brutus's sighing expression of the hope that he could know the end of the day's business 'ere it come'. But they already know that the assassination of Caesar was undertaken in vain. They are weary and resigned men, with no longer any sense of public policy (if indeed they ever had one after Caesar's death) and only a sense of private doom. Yet somehow the two friends, in talking together for the last time, sound in their elegiac tones of sad foreboding touchingly human, and more appealing than the two together have ever sounded before. It is not that we are invited to admire failure more than success; it is rather that the mixed motives and impulses which brought these two men together in an illogical and ill-starred political murder in the end reveal to us with moving clarity something of the moral and psychological ambiguities of human character and behaviour. Shakespeare has manipulated our feelings this way and that in displaying before us both Brutus and Cassius. He has a few more scenes to show before the question of how and in what sense Brutus might be considered a hero of the play can be resolved.

The battle ebbs and flows across the stage, as it could on Shakespeare's stage in a way it could not on the later specifically defined picture-frame stage. We see Cassius sending Titinius to find out if a distant body of soldiers are friend or foe, and when he sees Titinius surrounded by those soldiers he jumps to the conclusion that he has been taken prisoner by them and falls on his sword, held for him by Pindarus. It is the same sword that helped to kill Caesar, as he says in dying. His misreading of Titinius's situation (we soon learn that it was friends, not enemies, who surrounded him) was part of a death-wish, as Titinius realizes when he returns to find him dead. 'Alas, thou hast misconstrued everything!' It might be a motto for both Brutus and Cassius in the play as a whole. Titinius follows Cassius's example and kills himself, and Brutus, returning from success in his part of the field to find them both dead, exclaims with unconscious irony:

> O Julius Caesar, thou art mighty yet!
> Thy spirit walks abroad and turns our swords
> In our own proper entrails.

The irony lies in the fact that Brutus had persuaded himself, as a condition of his being able to join the conspirators, that he was out to kill the spirit of Caesar rather than his body, the killing of the latter being unfortunately the only way of killing the former. In fact, of course, he did the precise reverse of what he intended. The body was killed, the spirit survived.

Brutus's address to the dead Cassius begins in the noble tones of a public funeral oration, but turns almost immediately into something intensely and movingly personal:

> The last of all the Romans, fare thee well!
> It is impossible that ever Rome
> Should breed thy fellow. Friends, I owe more tears
> To this dead man than you shall see me pay.
> I shall find time, Cassius; I shall find time.

He will not mourn formally in public; his grief is essentially private (which is to say, in terms the play has established, it is real). The rocking repetition of the line 'I shall find time, Cassius; I shall find time' takes us into the depths of the grieving person, as opposed to the public spokesman. At the same time, as the movement of the play has already implicitly suggested and as its outcome, so soon to be revealed, confirms, he is not telling the truth, for he will never find time. His time is too short, and he will be dead before the opportunity of indulging in private grief for Cassius can come to him. There is a special sad irony in the fact that in this, perhaps the most movingly honest single line spoken by Brutus in the whole play, he is in spite of himself speaking an untruth.

Brutus returns to the battle. His companion Cato, with no more slogan left than the proclamation of his own name, dies fighting, while Lucilius, proclaiming himself to be Brutus so that the enemy would concentrate on him and leave Brutus unharmed, gets himself captured. There is something curiously barren and hopeless in the cries 'I am the son of Marcus Cato, ho!' and 'And I am Brutus, Marcus Brutus I', as though all they had left was their own identity (not even this in the latter case, since it is Lucilius pretending to be Brutus) and they no longer knew the public cause for which they were fighting. Brutus returns with his 'poor remains of friends', knowing that he is lost yet refusing to flee. He is now totally in the grip of a fatalistic assurance of imminent death, and seeks to hasten his fate by asking several of his men to kill him. They all refuse, and their refusal produces Brutus's last speech:

Countrymen,
My heart doth joy that yet in all my life
I found no man but he was true to me.
I shall have glory by this losing day
More than Octavius and Mark Antony
By this vile conquest shall attain unto.
So fare you well at once; for Brutus's tongue
Hath almost ended his life's history.
Night hangs upon mine eyes; my bones would rest,
That have but laboured to attain this hour.

The self-consciously noble Brutus raises his voice for the last time. He flatters himself that in all his life he found no man that was not true to him (but was Cassius true to him when he manipulated him into joining the conspiracy?). He makes one last brief reference to himself in the third person ('Brutus's tongue'). But the tone is most of all one of utter fatigue. The balancing of private and public selves, the application of abstract moral logic to justify the murder of his friend, the realization that the elimination of a source of power without replacing it by another produced only chaos, have proved too much for him. He kills himself, as his very last words make clear, with more good will than he killed Caesar. That is not rhetoric, but an honest confession of earlier failure to relate judgement and feeling. By this time we are able to see that failure as bound up with much in Brutus that is admirable. He is a kind of hero, whose idealism and nobility and intelligence and kindness and generosity are curiously combined with his vanity and naïveté. and love of abstractions and tendency to theatricalize himself. He is at his best as husband, friend, master, in domestic situations, and at his worst as patriot and public benefactor. Yet we cannot separate these two sides of him and say that he would have been a more satisfactory man if he had one set of characteristics without the other, for as Shakespeare presents him within the unfolding movement of the play he is someone whose characteristics on both sides are intimately bound up with each other. The judgements we are invited to make on him are often implicit in the kind of verse Shakespeare has him speak on different occasions. It is when we hear the true 'Brutus music' that we see the true Brutus. Yet on public occasions that note is hardly ever sounded and, when it is, it emerges intermittently from a more formal and abstract style, what one might call the third person as opposed to the first person Brutus.

Julius Caesar, as has often been noted, is a rhetorical play, containing within itself a great many varieties of rhetoric. But it has other modes of speech too, notably the elegiac, and in the relation between the different modes—as seen, for example, in the relation between the different modes in the sections of Antony's funeral speech—much of the meaning of the play resides. Antony's last speech—the penultimate speech in the play—is a tribute to Brutus as 'the noblest Roman of them all':

> All the conspirators save only he
> Did that they did in envy of great Caesar;
> He, only in a general honest thought
> And common good to all, made one of them.
> His life was gentle, and the elements
> So mixed in him that Nature might stand up
> And say to all the world, 'This was a man!'

This is a quite different kind of speech from anything that Antony said over Caesar's body. He has nothing to gain from it, and tells the truth as he sees it. It emerges as a judgement, not an encomium. Its tone is quiet and almost epigrammatic, almost like an epitaph from the Greek Anthology. Yet there are overtones that perhaps Shakespeare put there for our ears, unintended by Antony. According to the psychological theory Shakespeare is using here, the properly balanced 'humours' within a man constituted an ideal character, and every editor of the play annotates this passage to this effect. Yet, having been shown the different aspects of Brutus's character, having heard the different tones in which those different aspects were voiced, having watched Brutus modulate from private to public character and seen him trying to impose abstract public forms on private feeling and finally doing the reverse and reducing a public cause to a matter of private feeling, we agree indeed that the elements were 'So mixed in him that Nature might stand up / And say to all the world, "This was a man!"' That is the trouble with man. It is very human to be mixed, and Brutus is very mixed and very human. In his mixture and his humanity, as in the very different mixture and humanity of Cassius and the even more different mixture and humanity of Antony, set beside the single-minded unmixed efficiency of Octavius, lies a central part of the meaning of the play. It is not a meaning that can be abstracted into a generalization.

Octavius has the last word. He replies to Antony's praise of the dead Brutus (and do we sense a note of impatience?) with the brisk

> According to his virtue let us use him.

He will let Brutus's bones lie honourably, 'most like a soldier', for that one night in his (Octavius's) tent:

> So call the field to rest, and let's away
> To part the glories of this happy day.

'Glories'? 'Happy'? We have already seen (in Act IV, scene i) the new rulers of the Roman world at work. If the result is to be called happy and glorious, one wonders about the price to be paid for efficient power. That Shakespeare wondered too is perhaps indicated by the fact that he was to return to Octavius and Antony and the fate of the Roman world in a later play.

A Note on the Text

The only authoritative text of *Julius Caesar* is that of the First Folio of 1623, which appears to have been printed from a revised acting script used by Shakespeare's company. It is a good text, and in quotations from the play this text has been used with modernization of spelling and some modernization of punctuation. (*The First Folio of Shakespeare*, prepared by Charlton Hinman. The Norton Facsimile, London and New York, 1968.)

Bibliography

Editions

New Cambridge Edition, ed. J. Dover Wilson, 1949.
New Arden Edition, ed. T. S. Dorsch, 1955.
The Signet Classic Shakespeare, ed. William and Barbara Rosen, 1963. (Contains selections from Shakespeare's sources in Plutarch and a selection of critical essays on the play.)

Sources

Shakespeare's Plutarch, edited by T. J. B. Spencer, 1964.
Narrative and Dramatic Sources of Shakespeare, by Geoffrey Bullough, Vol. V, 1964.
Shakespeare's Sources, by Kenneth Muir, Vol. I, 1957.

Criticism

Twentieth Century Interpretations of 'Julius Caesar', ed. Leonard F. Dean, 1968.

By far the most useful single volume of criticism of the play for the student. Contains 19 essays on the play by different modern critics, including Geoffrey Bullough, Northrop Frye, Harley Granville-Barker, Leo Kirschbaum, L. C. Knights, etc.

Shakespeare's Roman Plays, by Maurice Charney, 1961.
Prefaces to Shakespeare: First Series, by Harley Granville-Barker, 1927.
Political Characters of Shakespeare, by John Palmer, 1945.
The State in Shakespeare's Greek and Roman Plays, by J. E. Phillips, 1940.
The Problem Plays of Shakespeare, by Ernest Schanzer, 1963.

Index